How to Write a Story
and Sell It

by Adela Rogers St. Johns

How to Write a Story
and Sell It

Never Again (and other stories)

Doubleday

&

Company,

Inc.

1956

Garden City,

New York

HOW TO
WRITE
A STORY
AND
SELL IT

ADELA
ROGERS
ST. JOHNS

To Herbert R. Mayes

who knows more than anyone else I have
ever known about the subject of this book,
and for over twenty-five years has done his
best to help me find out whatever I understand about it.

How to Write a Story
and Sell It

1.

The title of this book is, to me, somewhat misleading.

I do not really know how to write a story. Nobody does.

As the source of an electric light is electricity, which Edison himself admitted he could not define, so the source of a story is something that can be identified only by the results.

But since from the day I sold my first short story when I was nine years old until today, at sixty, there has never been a moment when I was awake—and frequently when I was asleep—that I was not in the processes which lead up to writing a short story, it is highly possible that my experience may prove valuable to others and should be recorded.

Some years ago one of my sons asked me to tell his bride how to bake beans according to an old California Spanish custom handed down to me. I started in, and after the third "How much?" or "How long?" had been answered by my rather vague, "Well—you know—when it feels right—or looks right——" my son said, "Mother, your recipes are going to be no good at all to future generations if you can't do better than that," so I decided to make cookbooks for my daughter and daughters-in-law and did it by carefully going back and finding out what I did, how much, how long, and all the details. I must warn you here that my daughters-in-law themselves admit the results are not always the same and I have been a mother-in-law too long and too often to explain to them that it is because they will not take the time or the pains to follow all the little instructions, like saving the water the beans were boiled in to add to the pot instead of ordinary faucet water, and chopping the peppers very, very fine.

So my how to on short stories must be an exploratory journey over fifty years of a measure of success in that profession. Because I did not get my Hollywood High School diploma until forty years after I should have been graduated, and then it was given to me at an alumnae banquet as a gesture of friendship, I have been allowed to teach some short story writing at both Stephens College and the University of California at Los Angeles on the theory that accomplishment in the subject taught was equivalent to the degrees I didn't have. What I have to offer is the result of what I myself have learned by adventure, trial and error and application, with my inspiration all too often the howling of the wolf on the doorstep and the children's bare feet. It was never only my own living I had to make, thank God. There would have been easier ways, but they would not have been as much fun. It is my own honest opinion that writing short stories is more fun than anything except newspaper reporting, and sooner or later you get too old for that. Sooner, usually.

The chambermaid at the Wissahickon Inn, a delightful spot amid orange groves in the small university town of Redlands, California, where I have been holed up for some months trying to catch up on deadlines, stood in the middle of my room the other day and regarded me with extreme disapproval. She is a pretty little Mexican girl who wears a bright red skirt and golden poppies in her black hair and I was sorry to have caused this dark despair, which she soon made vocal.

"Madre de Dios," she said, "you make more mess than anybody else in the whole inn. Never have I seen so many papers on the floor. And I am not allowed—I explain to the housekeeper—I am not allowed to touch them."

"Heaven forbid," I said. "How can I tell when I might in the fourth version want a line—even a word—from the first? I can put up with them." As she went away with a final disparaging glance at the heaps of yellow sheets, I said, "Moreover, muchaha, did you but know it, that is a large part of How to Write a Story and Sell It." Because in the end you have to get fifteen or sixteen, or on rare occasions these days twenty-two or twenty-three, pages winnowed, sifted, distilled, rearranged, resequenced, repolished, and cut, cut, cut, cut out of those heaps, until at last you have told your story so that the editor of a magazine may buy and publish it in his magazine for the folks to read.

I am not interested in stories that do not sell and get published and read.

They are no good. All good short stories get published.

Writing is not writing until it is read any more than an airplane is an airplane until it takes off and flies.

The heaps of yellow paper are among the things I can tell you about how to.

There are others I have learned, some of them the hard way.

1. *What you have to say is always more important than how you say it.*

2. *Anybody can learn to write, but there are very few writers and always have been, and this I can explain as we go along.*

3. *Ninety-two per cent of the elapsed time on a short story takes place before you ever put a word on paper.*

4. *The short story equivalent of a nose for news, the ability to know a story when you see it, is the one thing with which a writer of short stories must be born.*

5. *An absolute Must is the training and development of the writer's memory, which is different from any other, and unless the aspiring writer can recognize it when I define it later he would be better advised to go looking for uranium direct.*

6. *The majority—I should say 85 per cent—of short stories are in some degree reportorial, they are sparked by something the writer saw, heard, felt, or read.*

7. *Therefore it is necessary to have a nose like an anteater for everybody's business, a rubber ear that hears what people say, a spyglass that sees what's going on, a keen faculty of observation for little things, all motivated by a burning, unquenchable curiosity about people.*

8. *All successful short story writers are utterly ruthless about where and how they get material. Nothing can be inviolate to them. Change it around so it won't be recognized, use it to benefit mankind, but the story comes first always.* Get it.

9. *Read, read, read, read. Read all the short stories ever published. Later I will include some lists of reading I advise any young or new writer to do—and what they've meant to me.*

10. *Right now, check your own story reactions to these ideas* . . . A boy's blue suit with two pairs of pants . . . A borrowed diamond necklace . . . A mechanic's afternoon off . . . An old lady whose most treasured possession is a moth-eaten fur tippet . . . A young man and woman who, as children, had the same dreams . . . A son who took his inheritance and skipped . . . A girl whose stepfather kept snakes . . . The longest walk in the world. . . . *If you do not within a couple of days react with some kind of a yarn about at least one of them, give up the whole idea. All of these made very, very popular and well-known short stories. Good ones, too, if one of 'em is mine.*

11. *There are no new plots. There are only new people, new treatment, new reactions, new locations, new times. But it is necessary to invent a good story to*

> *tell, because a short story writer must be a story-teller.*
>
> 12. *A professional writer will starve if he waits for inspiration, he must learn to combine spontaneity of emotion with sound technique to make the result read like inspiration.*

I copied too many of my sons' theses when they were in college to be able to bear footnotes. About them I feel as my friend Frank Sullivan does in his immortal essay called "A Garland of Ibids." So I will give you the titles and authors of the short stories in No. 10 right now as part of the general narration and hope you'll like it just as well as if I put little 1. 2. at the bottom of the page.

In the order in which I listed them above they are "Salesmanship," to me a great short story for all time, by Mary Ellen Chase. Maupassant's "The Diamond Necklace," as early classic. Edna Ferber's unforgettable "Afternoon of a Faun." "Miss Brill," by the late Katherine Mansfield. Kipling's "The Brushwood Boy," my favorite short love story. "The prodigal son," as told in the XV chapter of the Gospel according to St. Luke. "The Speckled Band," one of the best of Conan Doyle's Sherlock Holmes tales. "The Longest Walk in the World" by me.

Which puts me in very big company, and I include it because the idea was given to me, as I have presented the others to you. It was given to me by the genius who edits *Good Housekeeping*, Herbert R. Mayes. I was able to create a piece that millions of readers liked, which just goes to prove that I am a professional short story writer.

My father, who was a famous and dramatic criminal lawyer named Earl Rogers and whom you are apt to meet from time to time in anything I write, especially about writing, always told me to qualify a witness as soon as possible, so that the jury could and would value his every word. If he was an eye-witness who had seen it, bring that out at once. If he was a medical expert or a handwriting authority, qualify him as such quickly. This highlights the value of his testimony, my father said, and makes the jury pay attention. So I am now going to qualify myself to write a book under the title of this one, and I do not mind telling you that the unqualifiedness of some who write, lecture, and teach on this subject has been one of the things which have made me feel an old pro should have a word to say to those who want to write short stories, are writing them, or just taking a course in short story appreciation for the average reader.

Next to the sonnet, I believe a short story—a superior short story—is the most difficult and precarious of all things to write, the most demanding of all forms to follow. It has to burn with a pure, gemlike flame. True, a novel (I have written six or seven, only one of which I myself thought was any good) takes longer, but it has to be easier doing. You can stop to explain. If you feel nobody will believe any man could be such a fool about a girl like that Mildred, there is room to devote chapters to the man as a boy, to how he first met sex, how his grandparents felt about it, what he learned about it as an intern in the hospital. Dozens of scenes can be strung together to build conviction.

In the short story you have to be right the first time. Every word must count, not just the right word but the only right word. Half the sentences in a good short story could be made into whole chapters in a novel, they must do the work of whole chapters. "You men! You filthy, dirty pigs! You're all the same, all of you. Pigs! Pigs!" Sadie Thompson said in "Rain." A Russian novelist would make eight chapters out of that sentence. Maugham made those fifteen words do it. Made your hair stand up. But I think Somerset Maugham would admit that it was harder to bring "Rain" to its amazing perfection than to write *Of Human Bondage*.

Those who have tried know.

2. I am, as you have doubtless gathered by now, but this is for the record, a professional short story writer.

For over forty years I have made my living at it and brought up a large family to boot. While I have never been able to save a cent I was able to take such good care of my younger brothers, children, and foster children that they are all doing well and can return the compliment if the time ever comes when I need it, though I'm sure it won't, for I shall never go dry. With a big family you continue to be actively alive, emotionally alive, and more and more material presses in upon you from every side. Writers stop producing in their later years only because they have lost active touch with the life it has been their occupation to report fictionally, after having passed it through the spectrum of their imagination.

Giving my profession its due, I must confess that some people, most people, could have saved quite a good deal on what editors and newspaper publishers, with an occasional desperation interval in The Movies, God bless them, have been kind enough to pay me. But I just never could seem to. This stupidity about saving money is almost universal among writers, who seem to lose what little common sense they have, never much and the more brains often the less, at the mere mention of the word. This is, I fear, a sad pose in memory of those days when Balzac starved in a garret, forgetting that Shakespeare was able to retire at fifty-one and go home so he'd have time and leisure to write a good play for a change. Thank God he didn't live to do it, for a good play on purpose by the author of *Hamlet* might have been a great disillusion. The attitude of looking down from lofty heights on the commercially successful writer is either an alibi for the impotence of few ideas, or a front for the dilettante amateur who fears to put his work to a continued test, or a spotlight in which a futile critic hopes to strut his little day.

I remember the late great Alexander Woollcott, in the days of the Algonquin Round Table and the newborn *New Yorker*, saying to me that there weren't five thousand people in the United States who could appreciate a work of Art. When he became a big hit on radio and his own books were best sellers, he was educated to the point where he could count the millions who listened to and read him in addition to the five thousand.

As far as I know, all great writers, all good writers, make money, and while it is a nerve-racking and hair-raising way to do it, what isn't? Nor does the fact that some very bad writers who hit a popular vein, like Mickey Spillane for instance, prove conversely that good writers can't make as big potfuls as he does. Over the long pull they make more.

This must be understood in any instruction on how to write a short story. For writing short stories is a profession so pleasant, so rewarding, so extraordinary in the kind of life it not only enables but forces you to live that I want to recommend that those who have a spark of talent or the faintest conception of what a story is should spend some time and work and study trying to see if they can make it theirs. If they do not succeed, if they can write but aren't writers, if they have ideas but are among the few who can't learn to write, they can probably go into radio or television or advertising, as so many failures in the field of creative writing have done. Those are well-paid and exciting jobs, if the aspirant possesses a strong heart, steady nerves, and a thick hide. They are potent and powerful in their influence upon the world today, and the training and discipline of trying to write short stories will benefit everybody concerned.

As near as I can figure—because when my sister Jessie died and we broke up the old house and cleaned out the attic a lot of my early efforts went to the Good Will Industry along with Jessie's trunks full of lace and furs and baby ribbon—I have written and sold about two hundred short stories, more or less twenty or thirty, and had seven rejected. This is a fair average, I am told, though I have bitterly resented those rejections, especially the last one, about which I will tell you later because the editor was right. I have had stories published in *Good*

Housekeeping, Cosmopolitan, The Saturday Evening Post, the *Reader's Digest* (in which they call a short short story a "Drama in Everyday Life," and I will explain that later because it's very interesting), *Collier's,* the *Ladies Home Journal, The American, Red Book, Today's Woman, This Week, Country Gentleman, Snappy Stories, The Black Cat,* and *Young's.*

This will prove that I worked my way up from the minors and could hit big-league pitching.

Right now I should like to explain one thing. This is a record of my own work, a sharing of my experiences. To stop every time I express an opinion and explain that that is what I am doing, to put "I think" or "I believe" in front of explanations or conclusions at which I have arrived, will slow the whole thing up badly. So let me say here once and for all that this is a book which contains my opinions and conclusions and that I think and believe them or I wouldn't be putting them down here.

While I have loved doing my work, I have never felt I came within hailing distance of doing it as well as I wanted to. Up to this day, every time I mail a story I sweat it out through sleepless nights and aching dawns until I hear first from my agent, Edith Haggard of Curtis-Brown, a fine editorial judge herself, and then from the editor. I know the story I set out to tell and no story I've ever written has suited me.

Not long ago Jack O'Connell, the brilliant young editor who has engineered *Cosmopolitan's* impressive comeback, and I were lunching at 21, having one of those gab fests which can be invaluable, and Jack said that in looking things over it had occurred to him that no magazine successes had ever been greater than those of short story series built around one or two central figures. He mentioned the enormous popularity of Hiram Holiday, Paul Gallico's hero who swashbuckled through *Cosmo* for many issues. Of *Red Book's* Claudia and David. We checked the recently published *Saturday Evening Post Treasury* (it is) and it proved that George Horace Lorimer had built a lot on Peter B. Kyne's Cappy Ricks, Mary Roberts Rinehart's Tish, Arthur Train's Mr. Tutt, Guy Gilpatric's Glencannon, Irvin Cobb's Judge Priest, and even after his death they had continued Raines's Tugboat Annie and Upson's Earthworm Tractors. Also there had been *The American's* Scattergood Baines, by Clarence Budington Kelland, and Edna Ferber's Our Mrs. McChesney, not to mention such immortals as Sherlock Holmes, the best-known fiction character the world has yet seen who appeared originally in an English magazine, the Saint, and my favorite, Mr. Fortune. And of course Dr. Kildare, and Fu Manchu.

Readers loved these characters as though they were friends, they discussed them in a way that made you know for sure you could never convince them Judge Priest wasn't a real person living down in Kentucky.

Fashions in short stories sort of come and go. There had been an idea around in the recent past that people wouldn't hold still for series any more, but I have always been committed to the theory that human nature does not change much at heart and that what has been well loved once will be again, granting it is well done and has been adjusted a little bit to new times and conditions. So I was pleased when Jack, having just returned from a visit to Ernest Hemingway in Cuba—and I would like to know what Hemingway does to folks in the writing game because I never saw anyone who'd spent as much as fifteen minutes with him who wasn't rarin' to go forth and lick the world—anyhow, I was pleased when O'Connell wondered if a series would be a good thing right now.

Also, I had an ax of my own to grind.

For over a year I'd been mulling over, sitting on, thinking about, when I was driving or listening or watching a ball game, a series of three stories around the temptations of Jesus as related in the IV chapter of Matthew. For it says that He was tempted in all points like as we are, which must mean that *every man that cometh into the world* sooner or later will have to face in some way those same offers that the devil made to the Man of Galilee in the wilderness. I felt they would be very dramatic and—moving if they socked a young criminal lawyer. Of course any young criminal lawyer I would write about would develop out of my vivid, vital young memories of my father with some up-to-date touches from my son Richard and my foster son Victor, who had just graduated from Stanford Law School. For all the characters a short story writer draws come from living people. Anyone who is interested in short stories should get this firmly fixed in his own consciousness, remind himself of it night and morning, so that he will never fail in observing everybody he meets all the time.

The hum and gaiety of 21 went on around us, people stopped to chat, waiters kept putting things down and taking them away, probably the perfect place to talk story, maybe as perfect as the Mermaid Tavern or the Cheshire Cheese or the old Jack's on Sixth Avenue. We are apt to let the past glamorize things and overlook our own atmosphere, and no writer can afford ever to miss so much as a whiff of atmosphere. His whole life consists of filling and refilling and keeping full his inner reservoir. In this stimulating atmosphere O'Connell and I got excited about my series and he suggested none too politely that we quit horsing around and I go home and write it.

This, let's face it, always happens.

Just when you are having such fun, talking about a yarn, somebody says, *Write it.*

So I boarded the next train back to California—this was just before Christmas—and chained myself to my typewriter, lit my prayer candle, and started to work.

Now this is told here to demonstrate beyond any possible doubt that there is little chance of any professional writer possessed of any honor, humor, or honesty ever getting a swelled head or falling into any trap of egotism or self-satisfaction. Humility has to pervade the very air you breathe. I remember once Marie Dressler said to me, "Life is always knocking me to my knees, but after all that's the best position in which to pray." Writing short stories is always knocking you to your knees until at last you find yourself all plowed up and broken up and humility can come in and light the prayer candle inside as well as outside.

When I finished the first of the temptation series I liked it as well as I have ever liked anything at that stage.

O'Connell didn't.

He said I took too long getting into it, I had let a minor character, a drunk named Killian, steal the story from my central figure, the young criminal lawyer we were supposed to be writing the series about, and that the girl was always off stage.

This all turned out to be valid.

I rewrote the story four times.

Finally, in the version that opened with a scene between the lawyer and the girl instead of one between the lawyer and the lovable drunk named Killian, it stuck.

The second one took me almost five months to write. If I could tell you why, it wouldn't have taken me five months. I can't remember ever having so much trouble before with a short story in my whole life. I had the people. They had all been in the first story, or most of them. I knew the story I wanted to tell and I wanted to tell it. By that time I had practically fallen in love with both Ernie Galan, the young criminal lawyer, and old man Killian. But it wouldn't jell. I couldn't find the line, I couldn't see it happening. I remembered one day when Bud Kelland came by for a cup of tea after a golf game when we were neighbors on Long Island. He was cranky as a plucked goose so I knew he was having story trouble and I asked him and he said, "I've got the guy out on the sidewalk and the girl on the porch and to save me I can't get him through the gate and up there." I couldn't get anybody anywhere.

This, boys and girls, is hell. To soft-pedal the fact would be to deceive you and lead you up a garden path. It is the short story writer's hell because, as I have said before, short stories have to be right. You only have so many words to do it in. If you flub-dub and fiddle-faddle around you will not have a short story.

Finally, I hollered for help. My good friend John Reese, who has sold more short stories to *The Saturday Evening Post* in the past two years than any other writer, lives not too far from me, and I went out to his house and we sat in his rose garden and talked all one night and half the next day. If there is someone to whom you can talk, it's a great help. Bounce it around. Hear yourself saying it. Try telling it instead of writing it, because you are primarily a storyteller, as the minstrels were, and while the written word is different and I have never known a good writer who dictated anything printable, the story line can be the same.

I went home and wrote the story I'd told, and this time it was okay on the first round.

The third one wrote itself, as the saying goes. It flowed. In a week I had a final draft done. Then I called Jack O'Connell, on the phone in New York. I said, "I have finished 'The Third Temptation.'"

He said, "Good."

I said, "It stinks."

He said, "How would you know? You wrote it. Send it to me and we'll see if it does or not."

It didn't. I got a wire saying, "Kay and I [Kay Bourne is the fiction editor of *Cosmopolitan*] are plain nuts about 'The Third Temptation.' By far the best of the series and we think the best you've done in a long time. It's a good thing writers have editors. Jack."

I still think it should have been better.

This, more or less routine in a pro writer's life, shows how little chance one of them has to to get uppity. You don't know what you're doing, you are rarely a judge of what you have done, you hash up a really good idea, a *really* good idea, and have to junk it for months. Every short story you write could be your last. An exciting challenge, but not conducive to egotism, conceit, rodomontade, or megalomania.

Hidden in my desk is that old beat-up book that every writer has, that everyone who hopes to write short stories especially must keep faithfully and take out every night before he goes to bed. The old notebook. In mine are several I have already written. Such as—Evie, the mother who adores her teen-age son but hates him because he looks like his father who broke her heart . . . C.B. selling the old family home . . . The night before D.'s wedding . . . Vic's article on will in the S.L.R. will contest around someone like H.'s grandmother, old Donna M.A.O. These have been sold and published.

Now there are about two hundred to go.

June and Willie—how could it have been so important then and so unimportant now? . . . The three men on the bench at Veterans Hospital at Sawtelle the day I went with I. to see her husband . . . C.'s sister-in-law selling C.'s mother's furniture at the auction . . . Going steady the time K. was in bed with the ankle he busted trying to stretch a double into a triple and his girl came in for the tickets to the dance . . . C.K., the problem father and his sons' marriages . . . The W.s' everything outside looks so smooth and easy yet they have the most terrible problem of any couple I know . . . The bad check a kid gave B.S. and the way the blond gal fought him about it that day at the Sherry-Netherland . . .

Reminders.

There should never be a day without an entry of some kind.

The eternal optimism that makes a gambler think he'll clean up on the next race keeps me believing that one of these will turn out to be the great story I've always felt I'd write someday.

All this is true, as far as I have seen, of every writer of integrity. A man's reach must exceed his grasp. We are the only ones who know what the concept was, what we meant to say, how far we came from reaching it. Dorothy Parker, whose every short story seems to me a polished gem, whose "Big Blonde" and half a dozen others seem to me without flaw, feels the same way about her works and threw away as not good enough as many stories as she has had published. Once she took my breath away so that I never spoke the rest of the evening by telling me—and our Mrs. Parker is famed for her devastating truthfulness—that she felt if she had my ability to put emotion on paper she might amount to something! The next morning at breakfast I suddenly burst into tears, and when the children demanded to know what was the matter all I could say was, "*Dorothy Parker* likes my stories!"

However, as to qualifications for writing this book, my stories, whether I am satisfied with them or not, and my way of writing them have been successful in the top bracket with editors, critics on the whole, and especially with readers. Mr. Hearst (William Randolph), by far the greatest editor I ever knew, once remarked to me, "Sometimes it seems that nobody likes the Hearst papers but the public." Times when I find myself left out of anthologies, though I know one story of mine, "Never Again," is better known and more highly regarded by the public than many that are monotonously ever present; when John Howard Lawson is given space in The Reader's Encyclopedia and I'm not; or when I read supercilious articles on the "slick magazines" written by pretentious failures and published in intellectual weeklies when my feelings get hurt and I have consoled myself with the same thought.

Last year *Good Housekeeping*, whose fiction has consistently reached heights with such writers as Daphne du Maurier, Margaret Cousins, Libbie Block, and (until he laid that dreadful egg with an AA story so inaccurate it didn't seem possible) Richard Sherman, published twelve short stories of mine and the readers were very pleased, so they wrote me. One month I just happened to hit *Good Housekeeping, Reader's Digest, This Week,* and *Collier's* all at the same time, and this adds up to more readers than any best-selling book of our time. Usually I get my name on the cover, which as a qualification means I am supposed to have "a following" who like to read what I write.

All this fills me with profound gratitude.

For, as I have said before, you are not a writer unless you are read.

Which brings me to two questions that must be answered, two questions I am most often asked by eager-beaver students of how to write and sell short stories.

Nobody but a fool would start a tough prospecting trek if he'd been convinced there wasn't any more gold in them thar hills—and fools cannot write short stories. Oddballs, crackpots, and madmen, yes. Fools, no.

Nor is anyone apt to succeed at anything if he starts on the premise that his best is too good, so he won't strain the last tissue to give it.

Short story writing is a tough racket. Like a doctor's, or pro football, or the FBI, or being President of the United States. The difference between being able to write, learning to write—which anybody can do—and being a writer is guts, stamina, discipline, endurance, dedication, the ability to absorb punishment, and working at it twenty-four hours a day, always conscious of it, always having it going on inside no matter what is happening outside, when you're awake and when you're asleep, because it keeps going on and often you wake up with a scene, a character, a solution for a plot tangle or a way to shorten your telling that you didn't have when you closed your eyes.

A long time ago, at a party Billy Seaman and Mayor Jimmy Walker were giving in their famous downtown apartment, I found myself dancing with a slim, curly-haired young man whose dark face seemed to me the most sensitive I'd ever seen. I didn't know who he was and vice versa until someone dancing by us said, "Hello, Adela," whereupon he stopped in the middle of the floor and said, "Are you Adela Rogers St. Johns?" I admitted it, and he said violently, "I've always wanted to ask you, do you believe all that sob stuff you write for the papers and magazines?" I said I did, every word of it, and he let out a crow like Peter Pan and said passionately, "I knew you did. I knew it. You have to believe it to make other people believe it. Like Al Jolson, when he gets down on one knee and sings 'Mammy,' he believes it and that's why audiences go crazy. I believe it, too. Whatever I do. The people who don't believe, they can never do it."

I was a lot more impressed by this when I found out that my dancing partner was George Gershwin.

Yes, you have to believe it. You *gotta give*. Everything you've got, all of yourself. Nor does the fact that what you have to tell is comedy, or gentle love stories, or murder and sudden death, you have to care so much they have to be written. No one has ever poured more of himself into a short story than James Thurber does into those fact-fiction tales of early years with his family. If I had to take one modern short story as tops—and I hate to do this because I loathe everything else he has ever written no matter how many prizes it wins—I could take William Faulkner's "Turnabout." He didn't write that one. He bled it. This is no journey for a frail bark and a timid pilot. *You gotta give.*

There have always been misrepresentations and sophistries about the short story field and they must be met before anyone can enter it wholeheartedly, and if not wholeheartedly nobody will stay the course.

So let's take up the one about your best being too good.

And then my conviction that there never is a time, never has been, never will be, when good short stories will not find publication. The only thing that could shadow this would be failure to get enough good stories.

3. Recently a student reported to me that the professor in a creative writing course at a highly respected university had said for all his class to hear that "the best writing in the United States has never been published."

This is not an isolated viewpoint, and I suppose it will always be found wherever there are sterile and frightened professorial minds.

Nevertheless, it is, of course, pure academic hogwash.

Many of the creative writing courses, such as the one taught at Stanford by that fine novelist Wallace Stegner, at Columbia, where the best writers and editors in New York come to lecture, and from my investigation in many of the junior colleges, are fine and honestly helpful. But truthful reporting compels me to say that too much inaccurate and prejudicial balderdash comes out of the ivory towers. There is sometimes a tendency on the part of the man who teaches what he can't do himself to belittle the man who can instead of taking advantage of what the man who can knows and has proved. Good teachers teach how to build bridges from bridges. Ones that have stood up. In the world's history there has never been a time when good writers weren't needed badly, as America needed Tom Paine and Harriet Beecher Stowe, as England needed Dickens and Bernard Shaw and France Rousseau and Voltaire. To see eager and courageous and talented youngsters made the victims of such poison gas as the above crack about the best writing has to infuriate any fair-minded writer.

I hereby challenge this professor to come up with one unpublished piece of writing to prove his open statement to a class of aspiring young authors. I am a busy professional writer whose spare time has to be spent in trying to help the White Sox win a pennant and the youngest St. Johns grandchild, whoever it happens to be at the moment, to walk, and teen-agers to think about the God, who created light in the first place, but I am willing to try to compose a board to read and judge such unpublished material. A board, say, of the best critics in the country, Clifton Fadiman, Harrison Smith, editor of the *Saturday Review of Literature*, the president of Harvard, Dr. Pusey, and Carl Brandt, dean of literary agents, who for many years saw to it that the not so dusty efforts of one Edna St. Vincent Millay got properly published. And in this connection I would like to suggest that everyone interested in writing as such read the *Letters* of Edna Millay, and see therein her own story of how eager her publisher, Harper, was to publish the best writing they could get their hands on and to what lengths of time, thought, attention, and money they went to accomplish same.

No matter what old trunk it should be dug out of, how young or raw or brash the author might be, how unknown to fame, I guarantee that anything this board calls the best writing will be published. By any magazine in the United States and at once.

No, no. The difficulty is that because of this kind of defeatist propaganda the best writing doesn't get written. I receive thousands of letters from aspiring writers. Some very young, and right now hundreds from women in their early forties who have time on their hands because all their children have married and gone away and who ought at least to have something to say. A majority of these seem to think they must write beneath themselves if they want to sell anything, that the first rule for selling a story is to write it for sale.

This is never true at any time in anyone's life.

A young man came to me recently sent by a friend to whom I owe so much love and gratitude that I would see any number of young men who want to write short stories. This one was a personable fellow, in a neat blue suit, brisk and businesslike. His proposition was that he wanted to make twelve thousand dollars a year and he understood that short story writers often did. To this I agreed and I asked him if he had ever written a short story and why he had chosen short story writing as his own means to this golden goal. He said he had written one short story about a trip to the moon, that he wrote letters which sent his friends into convulsions, and that he had heard that anybody could learn to write as well as necessary nowa-

days. He had a job and he figured in his spare time as a favor
to our common friend I could teach him all he needed to know
to get published since obviously the ebb was low.

I said there was rather more to it than that and he went
away.

When I reported this to my friend, the friend said, "Ah,
he had a button and wanted you to sew a shirt on it," and I
said, "I shouldn't in the least mind sewing a shirt on a button
if it was the best button somebody had. But to start with an
indifferent button is asking too much of anyone."

The other day a charming, highly intelligent, very well-
educated young woman brought me a number of short stories
which had been consistently rejected by magazines—many
magazines. She couldn't understand why. Reading them, I
could, and I was stunned. Her conversation had showed me
humor, tears, excitement, indignation, and strong reactions
to most things. I knew she was willing to work because she
had done a long, difficult job of research for a friend of mine
and made swift, condensed reports. Therefore it amazed me to
find her stories as stale and unprofitable as yesterday's toast.
Tired old plots (there aren't many others any more to speak
of, and we'll go into that later), unrelieved by characters who
walked off the pages as real people to make me feel with, for,
or agin 'em; or any brilliant or honest or important shift in
viewpoint; or any real or amusing dialogue of wit or woe; or
any fascination or glamour or newness of background to make
these old plots new. Never, as she moved her wooden pegs

across a dim checkerboard of limp nights and days, was there any indication that the writer gave a hoot one way or the other what happened to anybody, and there was no reason why she should.

It reminded me of the only time Paul Gallico ever had a spectacular failure. He wrote a story about a strike. As we finally agreed, it was a hell of a strike. But it didn't *happen to anybody*. On the other hand, in the best story about a strike ever written, Jack London's "Valley of the Moon," the strike didn't happen until the story was two thirds over, and then it happened to Saxon and her husband and their baby who was about to be born and the man and his wonderful wife next door and you cared like crazy. Storms, floods, fires, wars, birds have to happen to people you care about in some way, maybe only to laugh at, maybe you want to see them hanged, but they have to happen to people you have some interest in. Have to.

What really appalled me about this young woman, and it is a common case and so must be dealt with, was that she wasn't writing from life, from things in life that had started her imagination on the glorious fictional path of creating a new world peopled with her own males and females after the pattern of real humanity, sparked by her own emotions. She was writing from writing, as in the dark days of motion pictures a few years ago the studios were making movies not from life but from other pictures, and thus playing to empty theaters. And not even very good writing, but only any writing that had sold. She wasn't out there playing football because she had a desire to play or even liked to play football, or had a gift for passing or kicking a football, but because she hoped someday to make a pro team and a living and hear thousands cheer.

This—and I beg you to believe me—is never enough.

Never.

No matter how lousy the story that was sold, I know it was the best the writer could do and behind it lay some honest impulse. And when the editor can't get enough of these to fill twelve issues of his magazine a year, he folds it up, as a very good and necessary magazine called *Today's Woman* folded not long ago—for that exact reason.

I said, "You have to be bright enough to realize that if any of them were as bad as yours—and I haven't read any that bad in print myself—it was because the editors who have to get out a magazine every week or every month couldn't get anything better. These were probably short stories they bought to fill up an issue where they had big non-fiction features that would sell the issue and hold the readers. Don't you know that any editor who could get another Ring Lardner to write another 'Champion' or 'Golden Honeymoon,' or another Runyon to start more *Guys and Dolls*, or another Edna Ferber to come up with another 'Gay Old Dog' or 'Old Man Minnick,' or a new Fannie Hurst to do a new 'Humoresque'—any editor would be the happiest man in the world and would buy them at once and pay the highest price for them?"

She looked bewildered.

I said, "Let's take a look at any current issue of a good magazine."

God was kind to me. I pulled down from my table *The Saturday Evening Post* of May 7, 1955, containing a fine story by Paul Gallico and a good one by John Reese, but above all a long short story—now called a novelette but actually about the same length as the immortal "Man Who Would Be King," by Rudyard Kipling, which is always listed as a short story and published as one in short story anthologies—by Philip Wylie called "The Answer."

Evidently the editors responsible for fiction, Ben Hibbs, editor in chief, and Erd Brandt and Stuart Rose his fiction specialists, felt this was a great event and/or they were doubtful or nervous about printing so unusual and spiritual and different a story. Maybe both. Anyhow, they listed it on the cover and surrounded it by extraordinary praise from Bernard Baruch, Milton Eisenhower, Eleanor Roosevelt, Norman Vincent Peale, and Carl Sandburg. They both built it up and protected it by the endorsement of such names and such sentiments as Peale's " 'The Answer' is a unique and strangely moving story. With consummate skill, Philip Wylie has dramatically stated one simple truth that can save our world. It is hauntingly unforgettable," or the great Sandburg's ". . . Mr. Wylie's 'The Answer,' reminding one of John Bunyan's *Pilgrim's Progress* or the myth of the Four Horsemen of the Apocalypse . . . there will be ministers and priests reading it from the pulpit as better than a sermon for this hour of human destiny." Thus this magazine, with its large and solid circulation, made "The Answer," a short story, as important as anything it has printed since Whittaker Chambers' factual *Witness*.

Nothing could be a better example of what a fine short story will do and what its value to editors is.

I said to my little writer, who had been trying to write down to the slicks, as the writers who seldom appear in them call magazines printed on quality paper, "Yes, sometimes bad stories sell. Non-writers get printed because there aren't enough writers to go around. So many aspiring writers accept the line of least resistance and copy the bad instead of the good."

Bad stories, not so good stories, half-baked stories get printed because that's all an editor has to print at the time.

I can remember an editor who telephoned me one day in New York and in a most despairing voice said, "You don't have a short story you'd like to write for me in a hurry, do you? At this moment my inventory consists of one and a half short stories—the half is one I like the beginning of but the end is as futile as a dirty mop."

These not quite good enough stories which sell by accident or timing I sincerely believe are the worst thing that can happen to a new writer. The fluke of selling one lousy story is about all the gods are apt to grant him, and that can set him back for years.

But good stories always sell. All of them. One after another.

Great stories not only sell once but go on and on in every field and medium where storytelling exists. They also do for the reputation and standing of a writer what a grand-slam home run in the ninth inning of the last game of the World Series with the score tied does for a hitter. They become classics.

In the best book on all kinds of writing ever produced, *The Summing Up*, its author, Mr. Somerset Maugham, says that the first short story he wrote after many years devoted to the theater was "Rain." ". . . and," he says, "it looked for a while as though I should have no better luck with it than with those I had written in my youth, for editor after editor refused it. . . . but I no longer minded and I went on. When I had written six, all of which eventually found their way into magazines, I published them in a book." Everyone knows the brilliant success of the dramatization of this story as *Rain*, starring Jeanne Eagels. It has been and will continue to be replayed as long as there are legitimate theaters and motion pictures. It appears anywhere and everywhere that short stories can and in every medium where storytelling is the basic requirement.

Then there is "The Snow Goose," by Paul Gallico. If you want the full history of the writing of this truly great and glorious short story, you will find it in Gallico's *Confessions of a Story Writer*, which I have used with great success as a textbook. It *is* a textbook of short story writing if one knows how to handle it, teach from it, and explain it. Every teacher of creative writing in high schools, junior colleges, universities, and graduate schools should use it. It is a fine, careful, honest, warm, and intimate setting forth of how he writes and sells short stories by one of the best and most loved short story writers of our times.

But for now suffice it to say that after Dunkirk had filled his heart, mind, and soul with its pain and gallantry and prayer, Paul wrote "Snow Goose" and ran into a head-on collision with his editors about the ending as he conceived it. They wouldn't buy it with that ending, and in that anger and pain that comes with a rejection, especially an unexpected one, he at first would not consider their suggestion. What Paul has to say about it is a vital piece of information in considering how to write and sell short stories.

"I can well remember my thoughts and reactions while I wrestled with the idea of commercial compromise. Here was a piece I had written right out of my veins, and the magazine was suggesting that I dilute it for presentation to the magazine's readers. . . . There was more than the commercial aspect involved. There was the lingering suspicion that the editors might be right, not from the point of view of taste but from the artistic standpoint. A writer will rail and complain and beef about his editors and publishers, but I think most of us realize that if we were writer-editor-publisher all in one, with sole say as to what reached the public and in what form, a good deal of the output would be horrible. Pauline [his wife] and I reopened discussion of the story. She felt it would not harm it to make the change and let the love of the two principals be unrealized until it was too late, that it might even result in adding poignancy to the situation. I rewrote it in a night, sent it off by airmail and received a wire of acceptance within three days. I am satisfied today with the rewrite and the editorial judgment that asked for it. If it was a compromise, it was a successful one."

I do not think it was a compromise. Having read both versions, I am convinced that the rewrite is the better story. The truer story, the way it really happened. A writer of integrity, who knows the people of whom he writes with deep understanding, cannot re-create a compromise that is what those people would not do any more than a man under hypnosis can be made to do anything that it is not in his nature to do. You cannot, for instance, make a moral man commit a sin to which his soul will not consent. Nor can you make a good writer violate the nature and truth of those characters he has created out of his divine imagination, which is, after all, made in the image and likeness of that Source which first created man.

Both artistically and as a reader-pleaser, the final version of "The Snow Goose" was a sounder story. It went on in a small book to sell almost half a million copies—an outstanding and record-breaking feat for a short story on its own— to be done many times on radio, and the only reason it has not been made into a motion picture is that Gallico treasures it and will not sell the movie rights until he is satisfied that it will come to the screen as it was written.

Difficult as it may be to believe now, the first short story by Damon Runyon ever submitted to a magazine was rejected and by no less an editor than Ray Long, who then shared with George Horace Lorimer the top spot in the editorial world.

I was responsible for this catastrophe, and never in my life before or since have I been so scared, for at no time was Runyon a man to monkey with. The way it came to pass was my not minding my own business, a failing to which I am more prone than I wish, although in a way it is an essential part of my profession. Other people's business makes short stories, and how would you know about it if you didn't stick your nose into it? A short story writer must have the same 'satiable curiosity as the elephant's child. In the matter of Damon's first story I had an able assist from his wife Patrice —*Guys and Dolls* is dedicated to "P.A.G., who helped most," and the P stands for Patrice, so perhaps that included my co-operation on this one. For without us it is possible that no Runyon short story would ever have seen the light of day, an eventuality I cannot bear to contemplate. Nor can you.

At this time I was living with Damon and Pat at a hotel on Forty-ninth street near Madison Square Garden called the Forrest. It was just around the corner from Lindy's, where Runyon absorbed atmosphere, dialogue, and color night after night, and when the circus came to the Garden you could smell the horses and hear the elephants rocking back and forth in their stalls. At all times the noise and feel and smell and lights of Broadway were coming in through the walls and windows, so naturally Damon preferred it to any of the swankier spots, which had only the Plaza or Fifth or Park Avenue to hear and see. Broadway was as much Damon's short story beat as at one time the South Seas were Maugham's.

Pretty soon I became aware that Runyon was writing something besides his column and his coverage of sports events. He was still actually a sports writer, and when anyone interested in short stories realizes that Lardner, Runyon, and Gallico— among our greats, surely—all came from the sports pages, it's a wonder to me more young men who want to write them aren't clamoring at the doors of the sports departments. Damon spent a lot of hours at his typewriter without any explanation and certainly I wouldn't have dared ask for one. I loved Damon. Also I thought then and think now that he was the greatest newspaper reporter of all time. It was my privilege to work alongside of him—for instance we did the Hauptmann trial together, he wrote the news stories and I did the features —but just the same I was scared of him, as most people were. He had an impassive manner and an expressionless pan that were frozen over the biggest heart in the world when the chips were down, but I looked up to him and never interrupted him any more than a Little League center fielder would interrupt Willie Mays. So though I speculated a good deal and had a kind of hunch that maybe Damon was trying his hand at fiction, it took me a while to sort of hint that such might be the case. And even longer to suggest that I had made the switch from reporting to short story writing some years before and had a good agent named Leland Hayward.

Damon didn't even answer me.

One weekend he had gone up to Cambridge to cover a football game. It was a snowy, blustery weekend and late on Saturday I discovered that my typewriter had blown a gasket or had a puncture or something, and I was—as usual—trying to meet a deadline for Fulton Oursler, who was then editor of *Liberty*. I asked Patrice if I could use Damon's machine for a couple of hours. Reaching into a drawer for some copy paper, I saw a manuscript. On the cover it said THE HOTTEST GUY IN THE WORLD.

I know. You shouldn't read other people's mail, diaries, or any other written thing that is theirs. My grandmother taught me that many years ago. Nevertheless, I read that, and if you can imagine the temptation presented by what was obviously an original story of some kind by the hottest reporter in the world, it won't be too difficult to understand why I succumbed. Under it was another called BUTCH MINDS THE BABY. I read that, too. Then I went leaping and shouting in to Patrice and said, "Do you know that Damon is probably one of the best short story writers in the world? He is almost as good a short story writer as he is a reporter." I was babbling, but I felt a little like Balboa when with eagle eyes he stared at the Pacific and all his men looked at each other with a wild surmise upon a peak in Darien.

Patrice knew. She'd read them, of course.

But Damon was shy. He was, like a good writer, humble before his gift. He was uncertain and doubtful and—*afraid*. He'd told her that he was just doing it for fun, to amuse himself, for laughs, to get down some impressions. For goodness' sake, he wasn't a short story writer, he was a newspaperman. He wasn't a fiction writer, he was a reporter. He'd look pretty silly trying to write fiction, an old dog like him showing off new tricks. And actually it's interesting to realize that Damon was past fifty, that he was a top newspaperman before he ever so much as tried to write a paragraph of fiction. Which is also true of Lardner and Gallico except as to age—they were much younger, but they had reached the peak of their profession as newspapermen before they started to write short stories.

In one way or another, there is an apprenticeship to be served.

You have to have something to say.

This may come from experience or it may come from a passionate need to say something about everything you see around you.

When Pat had suggested to Damon that he ought to let an editor read one of his just-for-fun attempts at a short story, he clammed up as only Runyon could clam up. Like one of his own characters, which of course we all are.

But at that moment Runyon was several hundred miles and three or four days away. From Cambridge he had to go somewhere else to cover a contest of skill and science and he couldn't get back until Wednesday. That, Pat and I figured, gave us two days.

On Monday I took the stories to Ray Long at *Cosmopolitan*. On Tuesday he said he didn't think they were any good. They were, he said, too specialized to have any general reader appeal or identification.

Don't ask me why! I don't know. And later Ray Long, very red of face, didn't know either. I suppose the only answer is that editors, like other human beings, are fallible, they make mistakes, they may make an occasional mistake on any story by any writer. But their average is high or they wouldn't go on being editors. An editor should be able to be impersonal always, but no one still on this plane of existence can be wholly impersonal. Ray Long didn't like Broadway. He thought it was slumming. *Cosmopolitan* was then dedicated to grown-up love stories about people whose names would have been either on the society pages or in the top columns. It's just possible that in *Cosmo* the bloodhounds of Broadway wouldn't have been the sensational hits they were in *Collier's*, a weekly with a heavily male readership. Women don't like Runyon as well as men do. Maybe, as editor of *Cosmopolitan*, Ray Long was right.

But at the time I didn't think of any of that, believe me. I was strictly and personally in the bag. I had submitted another man's stories, having, to all intents and purposes, stolen them out of his desk; the one eventuality which had never occurred either to Pat or me—their rejection—had happened. While you learn in time to be philosophical about a rejection you never learn to like it, and the first reaction is always bitter and usually explosive. The insult penetrates and burns.

Somehow I was sure Damon would know even if I tried to conceal it. I had worked with him so long I was convinced nothing could be concealed from him. Even if Ray Long didn't say a word, and nobody exists who doesn't say a word to somebody, Damon would only have to pick up one of the manuscripts to get a clue. Nothing for it but to confess.

This I did. Damon was very polite about it. I wished he hadn't been. He froze. His gray eyes were very cold and I thought they were cold resting upon me, his friend who had invaded his privacy and subjected him to the worst. Soon I found out they were cold about the rejection of his stories. He had said they were just for fun. He had said he wasn't a short story writer. But it turned out he didn't propose to have anybody else agree with him. He was a fighter.

Later he took some stories over to *Collier's* and *Collier's* bought them.

The rest is legend and history.

In a fine collection of Katherine Mansfield's stories published by Knopf, her husband and editor, J. Middleton Murry, says, "Shortly afterwards, she finally abandoned music for literature. She submitted manuscripts to editors in vain, and, in her effort to make ends meet, she had varied and exacting experiences in minor parts in travelling opera companies and the like, until the quality of her writing was recognized by the

late A. R. Orage, the editor of *The New Age*." Who is remembered now because once he did recognize the quality of
Katherine Mansfield.

A peculiarly delicate quality. Not everybody's cup of tea, it
must have seemed. People. Little plot. Yet so poignant, so un-
utterably real and touching was Miss Mansfield's reaction to
what could happen to people, very commonplace people in
everyday life, that her success was great. No one can share the
quality of Katherine Mansfield's writing without being moved
as by few other stories ever written.

It took a while. But somebody did recognize it.

Somebody always does.

Or if there are exceptions they are so few that to say the
best writing in the United States isn't published is to state
a dangerous untruth.

Dangerous because I, for one, had a student at UCLA who
has the Katherine Mansfield quality. She can feel emotion
about poignant little things that happen to you and me, and
then she can get it on paper. She has an inner obligation
to write the best she can. One of her short stories was submitted to editors in vain, but they recognized the quality and
rejected the story only because it was dialect and not readily
understood. Now she, in order to make a living, has had to
take a job in social welfare, where there are a dozen stories a
day, and she is soaking them in like a sponge. To tell this
modest and humble child that good writing has no chance,
that her best will never be published, is to add a wicked burden

to the ones which already accompany writing at night after a long, harrowing day's work. The world might be robbed of stories like Katherine Mansfield's—and I'd be cheated of being remembered thirty years from now because I once recognized the quality of Joan Wixon's writing. Given encouragement, this girl can do it. But the your-best-is-too-good is a discouragement, it takes away from young and new writers the courage to try their wings at the highest level, and anybody knows that the lower you fly the greater the chance of cracking up and never reaching the destination marked on your map.

Now you will just have to believe that this happened right here!

At this exact moment my telephone rang, it being after three o'clock, when, if I am not so interested I don't get tired, I usually stop work and answer it. On the other end was a remarkable woman, sent to me by a professor at the University of Redlands, who has written a novel which may be over-zealous, too doctrinary to get published, but which showed me a great talent for hard-hitting writing, big thinking, and characterizations carved out of the side of a mountain. While she is sweating out hearing about her book, she has to eat so she decided to try short stories.

Quite cheerfully—she is a cheerful woman who believes in herself—she said, "I've finished one. I didn't like doing it, but I'm sure it's commercial."

The yell I let out could have been heard in Palm Springs.

"If you didn't like doing it," I shouted, "nobody will like

reading it. If you looked down your nose at it while you were writing it, I can promise you the editor will do the same. What is this? Who do you think you are?"

She said, "But you said——"

I said, "No, I didn't. I never in my life said to write anything commercial, whatever you think that is. I never said to write to sell. Never. I did say that it was no disgrace to use a little of the wisdom of the serpent, as Fulton Oursler used to tell me many years ago. If you are writing to put over a Cause, you will have to wrap it up and let the reader get it for himself. You will have to entertain your reader—or listener—as Jesus did when he told the parables, and the moral can't be rammed down their throats. But it is always fatal to write for the purpose of selling."

She had the guts to tear up what she'd done and go back to trying to tell the best short story she felt.

Somebody will always recognize your best work.

I had one shining example of this myself.

One of my stories which most of my readers always seem to remember and which newer writers always say they like and admire is "Never Again." Certainly it has been a great success. After I'd written it—I'll have some other things to tell you about that—it went to *Cosmopolitan* when Harry Payne Burton was the editor, and though at the time I was one of Cosmo's featured stars, Mr. Burton turned it down flat. A story about a girl who got drunk and killed her sweetheart was, he said, too realistic, brutal, and shocking to print.

The manuscript had been put on his secretary's desk for a return trip to me when a tall young girl, just come out of the West via Vassar, checked its flight into oblivion, for Burton's conviction that it wasn't printable was so strong that I, always very doubtful of my own work, would surely have dumped it in the nearest ash can. Miss Frances Whiting really thought it was a great short story, she recognized its quality when no one else did. In spite of being low man on the totem pole of the editorial staff at that time, she stormed into Burton's office and put up a real battle for it. She said it might be realistic, brutal, and shocking, but that it was highly moral and virtuous because it showed the hell to which drinking among young girls could lead. In this she was proved right later when many sermons were preached with "Never Again" as a text and the WCTU reprinted it in pamphlets. Her ability and personality later made Miss Whiting editor of *Cosmopolitan* in place of Mr. Burton, and she used all of them then. Burt MacBride, top assistant editor, backed her, and Burton reversed his decision and "Never Again" started its career, the latest chapter of which is its TV production by Alfred Hitchcock.

Somebody—in this case a junior editor named Frances Whiting—recognized the quality of the story which was the best I could do, the best I had ever done, for I had really given it everything I had in me, that one.

After I had leveled with the charming, intelligent, and well-educated young woman who had brought me the stale and profitless stories with the tired old plots, I asked her if there was anything she wanted to write about.

"You can't," I said, "have decided to write short stories just for success. Somewhere in you there must be something that has meaning, something you have your heart in. In the very beginning you must have felt you wanted to say something, to tell somebody something. Basically writing is a means of communication. Wasn't there ever anything you felt obliged to write, to communicate to other people? None of us can die on every cross, or fight on street corners for every cause, or defy the world in the name of every injustice, but there must be one thing about which you care enough to die and fight and defy or don't try to be a writer. You may shout to a merry tune, but you must care. What is it?"

She said the thing in life she cared most about was what was happening in the field of education. She had been a teacher, she had given it up because she felt herself defeated in her attempt to serve children by the present school system, she could no longer bear to see what seemed to her the supreme injustice of children being cheated of their right to learn by corruption and inefficiency. She loved children and hated parents and school officials and teachers who were lax and careless. As she talked, her eyes filled with tears and her voice quivered, her cheeks grew pink and her eyes flashed.

I said, "With all this inside of you, you go on writing tired old stories about a young wife cooking dinner for her husband's boss? Why?"

"Because," she said, and she did wring her hands, people do, you know, "because my agent told me stories about young wives would sell the women's magazines and no one was interested in education and not to write anything about it because it wouldn't sell."

In a controlled voice that felt like sandpaper inside my throat I said, "Did your agent ever hear of 'Good Morning, Miss Dove'? or one of my own about a schoolteacher named Miss Briggs and an apprentice jockey? Not to mention that there was and always will be, praise God, Goodbye, Mr. Chips."

With flags flying, she is now trying to write her best story about a schoolteacher's fight for a boy who ended up in junior high knowing almost nothing about anything because they'd always passed him anyhow. About this story, she cares. It ought to be good. If it is, it will sell. But meantime she has wasted two long precious years writing down to the market.

A very bright girl said to me the other day, "You know my sister and I have a one-room apartment and she's been ill, so I'm writing in the bathroom. It's not a very convenient place but I suppose it's appropriate, probably the stuff I'm writing ought to be written there and stay there—and maybe flushed on down. But I'm going to sell it. You watch. It's just about lousy enough."

I said, "You will never, as long as you live, sell anything that isn't the best you can do. Never."

And this I believe.

To write to sell is absolute and utter defeat before you have put a word on paper.

To accept prostitution of all that is the light that makes writing is death.

Writers may write mediocre stories and sell them, but they don't do it on purpose. There are just some people who write stories like that, and editors buy them because they need them and they have some degree of sincerity shining through the thin veneer.

No story has ever failed to find a market because it was too good.

Never.

Somebody find me one!

4. In the beginning when I planned to write this book—because for one thing it seemed simpler than trying to answer all the questions in all the letters or to speak to all the classes in high schools, junior colleges and universities, and all the writing groups in all the clubs, or talking to all the people who want to be writers whom I and my friends meet, and also because when I myself was teaching I found no adequate, practical, and inspirational textbook I could use and recommend—I planned the chapters on how to sell a short story at the end.

That part, I said to myself, will come last. Selling is merely mechanical.

How to write a short story is certainly more important than how to sell one, I figured. But while I was mulling it all over in my own mind, trying to find out what I really knew about writing short stories and how much of it I could put down in a recipe, I discovered that to 99 per cent of the people interested, how to sell is intrinsically part of how to write, for their stories are written to sell, and the writer sits back and studies his work and makes up his mind what will or will not sell, and how he writes and above all what he writes are much influenced by his conclusions on that point.

How to sell, I find, is in a way the preparation of the ground for the seed, and in most instances comes first. There seem to be two schools of thought on this subject. The small groups of budding, brooding, and illuminated geniuses who do not write to publish at all. And the much larger groups who wish to make a profession of writing and, since they have to have a roof over their heads or perish, must sell what they write.

Whatever the approach, it is essential to illuminated writing that it is written to be read. Before it can be read, it must be sold. Therefore, as good or bad soil in which that germ of an idea is planted and grows, it dawned upon me that selling a short story has to be considered first, which is perhaps only natural in an age of salesmanship.

This came as a surprise to me. Because I have never in my life written a story to sell, I have never, when I started a story, thought about selling it though I have always known it must be read or be a poor, frustrated, unhappy thing withering on the vine.

To say that I have never thought about selling a story—nor do I know any other successful professional writer who hasn't or doesn't—sounds like a bald-faced lie to many who know how carefully a pro writer markets his wares and how anxious he is to wring the last penny out of them in foreign rights, reprints, radio, movie and television rights. Thus it must be explored, and that is part of how to sell and again seems to come first.

Naturally, I have written short stories to order, for specific magazines, on special themes, for particular occasions like Christmas or Easter or spring or winter. This is not writing to sell. Do you think less of an architect if he agrees to draw plans for an office building required by the state one day, for a functional house the next, and for a small but beautiful church the day following that one? Of course not. He has to have a piece of ground on which to put the church with its spire that points a finger up to the sky and within whose walls men kneel in worship. It wouldn't indicate artistic integrity but perverse egomania if he insisted on building the office building where the owners wanted a church.

Violation of his artistic integrity would be in drawing plans for a church if he had no inspired conception of a church, if he didn't believe in God, if in his own soul he ridiculed God's house. Or if to please an owner and for money alone he drew shoddy, ugly plans for an office building, plans which tormented his architectural conscience and offended his eye for beauty.

Once Dickens had written "A Christmas Carol," the world wanted a new Dickens story every single Christmas that ever was. So Dickens, who loved Christmas and always had all his family, friends, and anybody he knew who had no place to go on Our Lord's birthday at his house, joyously wrote a new Christmas story every year and probably thought he was lucky to have the chance. This is not writing to sell, even though the stories were sold before they were written. This was simply the grateful joy of having an opportunity to do the thing a great writer could do best. Most writers can do some kind of story better than other kinds, and there is no reason they should not do that, once they discover it, any more than there is any reason why Nellie Fox should catch for the White Sox instead of playing second base, which he can do better than anybody else in the world.

In considering the preparation of the ground for how to write a short story, it is necessary to understand that there is a crying need for good short stories. Always has been, always will be. Make no mistake about that. Now is as definitely a favorable time for good—or great—short stories as has ever existed since the minstrels sang them in the great halls or Plato told such as the parable of the cave while wandering with his students amid the groves and gardens of the Academy.

If the short story market is off, as of course all markets are from time to time, there is usually one major reason. There aren't enough fine stories being written. All that ever is needed or ever has been needed to bring it back to buying peak is more good short stories. In the history of the short story there have always been ups and downs, changes of fashion, failures of magazines and reviews, basic alteration in trends and tastes, scarcity of capable editors, and one of the most interesting to all writers of—and readers who appreciate—short stories took place during World War II and in the years after it.

There was then a decline in the writing, then in the printing, and consequently in the reading of short stories. Reasons for this are plain to anyone who thinks about it for a moment.

First of all, there were not enough good short stories being written, so that an editor could depend upon them or make them part of his editorial plans and schedules. He had little hope of maintaining a high level of production in that field. The younger writers had been swept into service, many of the older ones were being used very actively in war work of some kind, women writers were busy taking the place of men, and moreover, most writers suffered a terrific emotional shock with the impact of the war and had little creative inspiration left.

Also, as was natural and inevitable, the war years placed enormous emphasis upon articles, factual tales so dramatic, so exciting, so absorbing, and so especially near and interesting and personal to every reader who had someone in the war—and every reader did—that nothing fictional could have compared or competed. Who could create personalities to compare with those who showed up every day in the headlines, or tell stories with the heart and soul of Ernie Pyle's never to be forgotten and immortal columns? Or the illuminated magnificence of Casey's Torpedo Junction or the action violence of Dick Tregaskis? All these things were for keeps, they were adventures with life-and-death stakes, their suspense was incredible.

Due to increased facilities of radio, cameras, communication, and transportation, the war happened right in our laps all in time, in broadcasts and newsreels. Impossible to believe that in 1813 Jane Austen could write *Pride and Prejudice* and never once refer to Napoleon or the Napoleonic Wars. In the second world war civilians in the United States were almost participants.

When my youngest brother was going ashore with the marines at Iwo Jima, his wife and I sat for three days listening on the radio to a play-by-play account that was as definite and clear as a football game. The 5th Marines made forty-five yards up the beach—they were thrown for a loss—time was out because it had grown too dark—I don't know myself how we lived through it, I can still see how my sister-in-law's pretty young face grew whiter and whiter until at last she was pinched into a small waxen image. I remember very well the day in a projection room at 20th Century-Fox when on the screen I suddenly saw my brother slogging up the sands of Iwo Jima exactly the way he used to ram through the line when he played halfback for Hollywood High. I thought my heart wasn't going to start beating again at all!

The gift of what is called "escape" writing is always rare and it had to be very good to hold during that war. We shall see that the vast majority of superior short story writers, including Kipling, Hemingway, Saroyan, Maugham, Katharine Brush, Irvin Cobb, Kay Boyle, Stephen Vincent Benét, Booth Tarkington, Jesse Stuart, Fannie Hurst, are all reportorial in inspiration and method. An Elizabeth Goudge, a Robert Louis Stevenson is an exception, and it's rather difficult to classify the good writer of detective short stories—Dorothy Sayers, H. C. Bailey, Sax Rohmer, Conan Doyle.

So the circle of supply and demand which had been spinning

higher and higher began to run down—little supply, little demand—until it almost stopped altogether. A few of the old pros who had learned to use technique when spontaneity and inspiration were lacking did the best they could, but obviously technique, valuable as it is, will never alone reach the top.

Then, ten years after the war began, four or five years after it ended, the situation began to change. It had to. Like the politician, the editor is nearly always a little behind the public; it takes him a while to catch up and find out what the public really wants. And what the public really wants in the end it can always get, of course.

Gradually the article field began to wear thin. Articles compared to those of the war days were a little flat. There just weren't enough to go around. They lacked importance and vitality, they were stretched and strained out of all proportion. Real life began to look, as real life sometimes does, sort of ordinary and drab; there was—since it is a fact that writers must be to some extent bound by facts—a growing sameness in them. For they had not been passed through the spectrum of the creative imagination of a fiction writer. They lacked the supreme appeal of reality, for after all, imagination is always the gateway to reality, since so many are blind to half they could or should see. Facts clutter a story, they have to be rearranged and organized and some of them removed. Only a fiction writer can do that, or in later perspective a true historian or biographer.

Also by this time only the least intelligent readers could fail to know "how to" do a large number of things, and while it was pleasant to be refreshed and kept up to date, the first strong appeal had worn off.

But the editor, to make the shift back to more fiction, had to get more fiction to make it with.

By 1950 the need was back, the demand was beginning to be felt by all but the most brash and stupid editorial minds.

The hiatus had left a gap and this had to be filled by writers who could write with some consistency of production. The great list of short story writers on whom George Horace Lorimer could count when he built the first success of *The Saturday Evening Post*, or that which was available to William Dean Howells when he was editor of the *Atlantic Monthly*, or to *Collier's Weekly* in the days of Chenery and Colebaugh, had to be replaced. One swallow does not make a summer, and an occasional short story which is just not too bad to be published doesn't make a short story writer.

When I decided to try to make *Cosmopolitan* magazine, back in 1922, I sent Ray Long three stories at once. I was advised to do this by Mr. William Randolph Hearst, for whom I had worked as a newspaper reporter. He said it would always impress an editor to know a pretty good short story wasn't just a happy fluke. He said it was rather like a rookie going up to the big leagues, the real experts never counted on much from his hitting until he'd been around the circuit the second time, after the pitchers had been able to figure out what he couldn't hit.

I hadn't hoped to sell all three of them, but I thought maybe they would show my good intentions and hard work and that consistency which remains a jewel in any field of productivity. Naturally, if nobody had ever heard of Stephen Vincent Benét and he sent in that masterpiece "The Devil and Daniel Webster"—come to think of it, maybe that's my favorite short story of modern times and certainly it's entirely the work of true creative imagination—anyhow, any editor would buy it, and if Benét had never written another he'd still have had the glory of printing it. But how many short stories as great as that can there be? So I was willing to show that I'd keep on trying if necessary.

Fortunately for me, Ray Long liked them all and was so pleased that I had written more than one that he began to pay attention to me and help me right from the start.

Don't forget this:

Talent is one thing.

Everybody is so smart nowadays, so well educated, has seen and heard so much more than ever before in history—we are moving up and up in our individual intellectual grasp—that there's a good deal of it around. Bound to be. But, as Gracie Allen once remarked to me when I said Frank Sinatra really had talent—this was in the days when he sang on the Hit Parade, "Oh sure. Almost everybody has. Let's see can he wrap it up." As you know, Frankie could and did. Some people with more talent whom I've known haven't wrapped it up. Talent plus hard work plus guts plus stamina plus constant prayer plus heart expansion makes genius. Or—go the other way. Talent minus hard work minus guts minus stamina minus constant prayer minus heart expansion makes people who say the best writing never gets published or who commit suicide young or hate editors.

You always have a choice if you have talent.

If you really want to know how to write a short story, it must start inside you somewhere with a conception that means producing more than one airplane a year, which it wouldn't pay to start a factory in order to do.

If you wanted to be a singer, you would know you might start with a voice, but you would have to go on from there and it wouldn't be much help if you could sing only one song once a year. It's always difficult for the professional writer to figure out why everybody is more or less convinced that he could write a book or a short story "if I only had the time." Often you gain the impression that some people think time is all it takes. It used to annoy me, but as I got older and less easily annoyed and more curious about why people think and feel as they do, I realized it was because it is true that all people have some stories inside of them, they have seen and heard events their instincts tell them would make great stories or incidents they can compare with books and stories they have read and be aware that their own experiences—if properly set down and put together—would have as much or more dramatic value.

I doubt very much if I have ever in my life been with anyone for an hour when I didn't get some kind of a story from him, either by words, impression, or plain osmosis.

But the person who wants to be a professional short story writer and begin to rebuild those old-time lists of which I spoke must have within his heart and soul a full conception of and desire for an all-time job. One that occupies his mind and imagination and memory all the time because it takes a great deal of material to fill the demand of short story writing as something that sells and makes a living.

To do this, it is necessary to be a short story writer twenty-four hours of every day, 365 days every year.

You can never get out of shape.

I thought of that the other day when I went out to watch the Los Angeles Rams begin their practice for the season. August. Ninety-four in the shade. It was tough. They were out of shape, they were unhappy about the weather because when you practice football you have to wear the works, pads and helmets and all, and with anguish, sweat, tears, and cussing, they began to fight their way back to being able to play football again. I was there—as usual—because it had occurred to me that nobody as yet has written what I consider a really good story about pro football, and there have to be some. As I watched them I thought, Well, one thing about being a writer, you never never get out of shape, you never quit playing, you are always practicing. If you go to your son's wedding you think he's a lucky man to get a girl with a disposition like hers; in the end a disposition is the most important thing in marriage—

isn't it—or is it health—no, a disposition—and of course it's been made so by nature that a young man never stops to think that he only knows how cute or not cute she is, and it's just luck if he gets a girl like Joan because, of course, it was because she's so cute but she has the disposition of an angel, likewise, and she'll probably need it because he's a darling but he's belligerent—always has been—how much do kids change that could make a story the mother who can judge because of something she remembers the kid did when he was six or seven—the lilies look pretty, they symbolize something that's not so important any more, purity, virginity, or is it—what about that story I've had kicking around for twenty years about Z.—the talk I had with her the night before—maybe it's time for it now—he's playing here comes the bride too soon—no, no he isn't—there's Aunt Minnie, I wonder how an old maid of fifty feels at a wedding, does she think she's missed the best thing in life or does she feel she's had it pretty good when she looks at Maude and realizes what Maude's husband is like about other women or would she be willing to—Ring Lardner did something like that in "Anniversary," but not about an old maid—funny, I can't remember what I wore at my first wedding, not a thing—it wasn't a wedding dress and veil, I know that much and I can remember the chapel and my father, exactly how he looked, can't do anything with that for years, father of the bride that's gone for good now and I can see his wife, what a beautiful gal she was, but I can't remember the bridegroom very well, not at the wedding—how many people can remember what right now is making the real impression on those two, or isn't anything—maybe they are seeing their past lives unroll as you do, they say, when you're drowning . . .

All this goes on inside and always there is a conscious interest in it because of short story pull and draw.

In time a great deal of that, for instance, went into a short story of mine called "The Longest Walk in the World."

It has to be like that all the time.

And one reason there are not ever enough good short stories written is because there are not enough good short story writers, and so you ask why, and one reason is that this big conception of all life as a large river pouring into the soul, the heart, to be let out when you open little doors—this one or that one—marked with a title—or an idea—is missing.

Then there is the excited recognition of finding the place to put a short story—and this comes as a joy, should come as a joy, and not as a narrow-minded egotistical resentment that maybe you ought never to think about where to put your story. There is an enormous difference between writing just to sell and writing with gratitude and a freer mind because there are magazines that buy stories such as you hope to write. There is no great merit in starting out from pure cussedness or contrariness to write something nobody wants to buy and then calling this artistic temperament or genius. That doesn't make any sense in art any more than it does in business. It would be a little silly to refuse to look at the Sistine Madonna because

Raphael painted it by order of the Pope for the church of San Sisto at Piacenza.

There are all kinds of magazines in this country. All kinds. Good and bad. They have a perfect right, morally and professionally and artistically, to declare themselves as to what types of stories they want to print, and it is, and always has been, a great convenience to the reader to know about this. The man whose major interest is sports has a right to know that when he buys *Sports Illustrated* he'll get stories about sports and not have to go fumbling around and perhaps end up with a magazine devoted to tatting or true confessions. This does not mean that within its declared limits of interest *Sports Illustrated* doesn't propose to publish the finest, most interesting, and well-written stories it can acquire. There may be in one block in your town three emporiums which sell things to drink. One is a gin mill, one is an ice cream parlor, and one is a hot dog stand with a beer license. If you want a tom collins you go into the first, and so on. But the man who wants a drink has a right to know that he can't get a banana split in that place. It's the same with magazines. They pretty well tell you what kind and type and trend of short story they have put a large amount of capital behind publishing. This is certainly their privilege. The reader can buy the *Ladies Home Journal, True, Esquire,* the *Lapidary Journal,* the *Oil and Gas Journal, Country Gentleman, House Beautiful,* or *Confidential* if it hasn't been removed from the stands for being against the public good by now. All this is for the sake of the reader—the purchaser—without whom the professional writer certainly cannot make a living.

But the writer has an infinite field to which he may send his story, and this is mentioned here because I think sometimes it is a comfort to feel the story has a possible home waiting for it. Maybe not. For some writers this is a help and reassurance. Others like to feel absolutely free of any restraint or restriction. So a new writer may write his story the way he sees it, feels it, without pulling any punches, and then determine where to sell it so others may read it. Or if it gives him a place to put his feet, he can decide he is writing it for a certain magazine. Anything that helps to get a short story written is permissible. Anyplace that the writer finds opens the floodgates, I don't care whether it's a tree house or a bomb shelter. Gallico thinks he writes best on top of an alp. I prefer the sound of the sea. Katharine Brush had an octagonal desk built for her by the great Joseph Urban and used to shut herself inside it and close the gate so she couldn't get out. *Write.* But it's not fair to squawk if a rough, tough story about the early days in Alaska such as Jack London wrote doesn't find a market in *Better Babies.* If I tune in to hear and see Dizzy Dean telecast a major-league ball game, which I do every Saturday morning, I have a right to see Diz and not *What's My Line,* though *What's My Line* is splendid if you are looking for a quiz show.

Remember with some small degree of gratitude and appreciation that if it weren't for organization and capital and all the modern conveniences the writer wouldn't have anyplace to get published. The pulps are fine, many of our best writers got their early training in them, they are like the minor leagues in baseball. On the other hand, don't allow yourself to fall into the error of looking down your nose at what some disgruntled soul designated as "the slicks." Just to see, I picked up this moment from the nearest shelf *Post Stories of 1936*. This contains Stephen Vincent Benét's "The Devil and Daniel Webster," which is included in most of the anthologies no matter how high-brow; a story called "Some Ways like Washington," by Booth Tarkington, as near the great American novelist for my money as Hemingway because Tarkington wrote about America and Americans and twice received the Pulitzer Prize for stories of America; my next-to-favorite Gallico, "Tightwad"; a Mr. Glencannon classic by Guy Gilpatric; a fine short story by the perpetual best seller, John P. Marquand, and the same by Mary Roberts Rinehart, I. A. R. Wylie, James Gould Cozzens, and John Taintor Foote, who wrote another that might well make my best ten—"The Look of Eagles."

No wonder I have that on the shelf where my hand finds it at once.

What an amazing volume.

How, where, when would these professional short story writers, all in the very front rank by any standards any time, giving their whole lives and every moment of their waking hours and attention and strength to creating stories, find the time and place and freedom to write such stories if a magazine didn't pay them to do so? Starving in a garret is all very well, but

eventually you collapse and then you can't write. I am sometimes dumfounded at the lack of gratitude and appreciation
that aspiring writers have for the work and investment and
constant vigilance on their behalf of the big magazines. Sure,
they make money, too. If they print good short stories it's impossible not to make money.

Right now they all need good short stories. The fact that
most of them are printing mediocre ones proves that—not
that they like to print mediocre ones, but they haven't any better and would welcome them. Any magazine, obviously, would
like to come up with the sorts of short stories in 1956 that this
1936 volume shows were published that year. Today anyone
who is willing to work, study, learn, live, sacrifice, write and
rewrite and rewrite again has an opportunity to help 'em do it.
It's wide open. The competition for a new writer, as you can
see by reading any of the magazines, isn't what it was if you
were trying to break in in 1936.

We now know fairly well how to sell a short story.

To sum it up, it turns out to be simple.

Write a good one.

There are no magic tricks.

You can't sell a bad story, you may get by on timing and luck
with one or two not so good ones, you will always without fail
sell a good one, and if you write a great one, everybody will do
nip-ups, believe me.

On the practical side, it is wise to have an agent because the
agent knows what magazines want what kinds of stories and

where the needs are just as any middleman does. Some agents—my own Edith Haggard of Curtis Brown, Ltd., Carl Brandt of Brandt and Brandt, Lurton Blassingame, Harold Matson, Harold Ober—to mention only those of whom I have personal knowledge and experience—are also competent editors themselves. *Editor and Publisher* and *The Writer* are invaluable for indications of market in great detail.

Yes, your manuscript will get read.

By editors, by agents.

Magazines, on the whole, keep a large staff of associate editors who do nothing but read. They aren't Beatrice Gould or Margaret Cousins or Betty Ragsdale of course. But they are all clever enough to recognize a good short story and they will seldom miss a great one.

There are naturally some not so capable editors. I have met up with a few. Fortunately for me they came when I had enough self-confidence to fight for myself, when I knew they were wrong and my children were old enough to go to work if necessary. The funny part of it is that I learned a great deal from the few incompetent editors with whom I had to deal. It taught me to clarify, to understand that I had to make it so good that even a bad editor couldn't miss it. It also taught me that editors have personal prejudices and likes and dislikes, and that if I am absolutely sure of my character or unfoldment of story I must stand on it. A bad editor can never convince you that something is wrong when it isn't.

Eddie Arcaro says great horses make great jockeys, but it is also true that great jockeys make ordinary horses win races they would otherwise lose, and certainly the ability of a great jockey has decided many a handicap. An able rider makes a difference to any horse. Great editors make great writers, great writers make editors look good, great editors can lift a fair-to-middling horse over the finish line by a nose, and under the editorial whip of a great editor writers run better races than they can.

There is only one way for you to find out about editors and that is to study their magazines.

Today editors do not have as much time to work with writers as Lorimer and Long and Max Perkins did and that's unfortunate, but then nobody has as much time for anything any more. To many writers interest from somebody is a very necessary thing, as an audience is to an actor. Out in a little foothill town in California called Arcadia there used to be a group of close friends composed of Harlan Ware, his brother Leon, John Reese of *Saturday Evening Post* fame, and their wives, Jim and Billie Cagney, occasionally Henry and Mary McLeMore, James H. Richardson and his beautiful Maggie. And me. Richardson is not as yet a short story writer but he is the ranking city editor of the Hearst service and wrote what Upton Sinclair regards as the best newspaper book of our time. These social gatherings always turned into jam sessions about short stories. Here we heard the first bare idea of Leon Ware's great story about the little boy who lived on the bridge, and John Reese's "The Girl He Couldn't Afford," one of my favorites. Out of intelligent, hard-hitting conversation and argument—

we were about 50–50 Republicans and Democrats for one thing—out of stories told of adult experiences and childhood, came ideas for yarns that we had overlooked or that maybe weren't for the man who told them but were for a listener.

This was strictly a pro crowd, of course.

We were lucky.

There is about as much ham in most skillful writers as in most skillful actors. If a young or new writer doesn't have editorial help and interest as yet, he ought to try to get it someplace. A wife, husband, friends, mother, father, teacher, somebody to exchange ideas with, someone who wants to listen and cheer a bit, someone who is waiting to read a story when you finish it, someone who cares whether you ever write it or not.

This is one of the real purposes—the realest, for my dough—of classes and schools of creative writing. I don't know how much you can teach anybody about how to write. The sound creative writing teacher can undoubtedly act as an editor, criticizing, telling a writer when he doesn't have a story or some part of it on paper, suggesting ways and methods of telling it. But to me the teacher's highest and most important function is to supply that interest. Writing is a lonely business, in the end it has to be done alone, but the interest someone else has is a magnetic force that helps to pull the story out—it is like the light at the end of a tunnel which assures you that there is an end and that there is light.

The first day I took over a new class at UCLA, I looked at

the assignment sheet I'd made from the morning paper and radio news, matched up assignments to reporters as best I could without any knowledge of their ability—but that's the way to find out about it—and said, "Let's go. Be back in here by twelve-ten and the deadline is one twenty-five." A complete, shocked silence met this such as I have seldom been aware of in a roomful of forty college students. I said, "What's going on?" and after a moment from the back of the room a small voice said, "She wants a story by one twenty-five." And then there was a sort of concerted *Whoop*. Seems that up to then no one had worked them on a fast newspaper deadline, nobody, as they explained to me later, had wanted their stories that bad. It started the old adrenalin working and they did rather well on the whole, and by the end of the semester were doing a real job. They all agreed that it was the deadline, the interest, the fact that somebody cared that pepped them up.

That was Ray Long's technique with me, and so Irvin Cobb told me with him. We were always Hopalong Cassidy riding to the rescue. Once Ray came out to California to persuade me to save the magazine because a certain set of short stories he'd ordered in England from an English writer had turned out to be flops of a sensational order. I nearly killed myself on that one and didn't find out until years later that Ray had known for months about the English stories.

The deadline I gave my students was simulated.

The writer can sometimes set himself deadlines of his own. And while a pro circle like the one in Arcadia may not be available at first, no circle I have ever seen fails to be interested in stories. Nor to any real short story writer should there be any circle that does not produce stories, if a would-be writer knows a story when he meets it. People are people; love, hate, murder, jealousy, faith, pain, failure, triumph, terror are common to all men and women. Look at the picture in the morning paper of the woman an ex-husband just killed another man over. Ten to one, she does not look like Helen of Troy or Marilyn Monroe or Grace Kelly.

All these things are put down here to indicate the importance of a writer's state of mind.

This seems to me something that is too often completely overlooked, and I can think of nothing more significant, more vital. Anybody knows how important the approach is to, say, an athletic contest. A football team is taken away the night before a big game, not for the reason of physical preparedness, because the team would probably sleep better in what Dizzy Dean, God bless him, calls their respectable beds, and probably they are, at that. But because of a state of mind, the "edge," the being together. A golf champion's state of mind is either good or bad, and sports writers will tell you much about the man's chances on the day of the match. Hogan's hot. Or Sammy Snead is off. Which doesn't mean his ability or physical condition has changed. It's his state of mind. An inner faith, conviction, will to win, desire about that particular tournament. Personally, I have always been fascinated by salesmen; selling is the one thing I am sure I couldn't do, but I should think success in this field would depend a great deal on the state of mind, on the warmth of belief behind what a man is selling.

For years I have treasured the finest definition of artistic temperament I've ever heard, given me by a great actress, Alla Nazimova. "You know those little Chinese bells they have in the doorways?" she said. "They are not what we call bells, they are panels of delicate glass, hung very lightly by silk cords. The merest breath of wind makes them tinkle, they respond to a stir of air you have not felt at all. That is the artistic temperament. It finds itself depressed or exalted, dark or illumined, and does not even know why. As you think back, it may be a letter, a paragraph or picture in the newspaper, a tone of voice of someone you love, a bird's song you didn't know you heard, a memory drifting across your soul. People without this sensitivity may be like the big brass gongs outside the temple, they must be hit with a great padded hammer to make any sound at all. But the little glass bells will give you music in response to a sigh, they will dance to a breath of spring. And they will break if the storm is too great—but not often. They are much stronger than you think, but they are sensitive."

Don't be ashamed of a lot of artistic temperament.

Without some of it, no one is likely to succeed as a short story writer. It isn't necessary to put on displays of it and get in other people's hair about it. However, between you and me, sometimes it helps. If it is on the level—nobody worth bothering about is impressed by a phony pose—I have found that other people, once they understand it, are both sympathetic and respectful. The average citizen knows that the artist—and a good short story writer must have some artistry in him, he is a creator—has that sensitive nature which really does make things hit harder.

Temperament is important.

Like fire, it has to be handled wisely or it can consume instead of warm and heat and produce birth.

The two most temperamental writers I have known personally were Katharine Brush and Dorothy Parker, though I don't mind adding that both Ring Lardner and Damon Runyon had their share! When I think of the way Runyon used to behave at breakfast in Flemington during the Hauptmann trial— which was a time when we all got temperamental at that . . .

To me, Katharine Brush's untimely death was not only a personal sorrow but one of the greatest blows American literature sustained in those years. *Young Man of Manhattan* and *Red-Headed Woman* in spite of their enormous popular success have never received the critical kudos they deserved nor the recognition of putting an era down on paper just as well as F. Scott Fitzgerald did in *This Side of Paradise* and *The Beautiful and Damned*. At her best as a short story writer, Kay Brush was tops. "Night Club" is as good a short story as you'll find, and "He and She" is a perfect example of sheer, powerful indirection as a method of telling a yarn. Artistic temperament killed Kay as surely as if it had been a gun fired at her head. She never learned to take writing in stride even a little bit, yet she could no more stop than she could stop breathing. They stopped together. A story took possession of her, her characters lived with her, ate her up, she loved and hated them in a way her suave, elegant, sophisticated exterior—Kay was a beauty and the best-dressed writer I ever saw—didn't lead you to expect. Working on a short story, which she liked best, was a long, painful delivery, too long, it turned out, for her to survive her creations. The passion her stories show is icy, but it is authentic passion.

Consuming fire destroyed Katharine Mansfield. After her death at thirty-five, her husband wrote of her, "She suffered greatly, she delighted greatly, but her suffering and her delight were never partial, they filled the whole of her. She was utterly generous, utterly courageous; when she gave herself to life, to love, to some spirit of truth which she served, she gave royally. She loved life—with all its beauty and its pain; she accepted life completely, and she had the right to accept it, for she had endured in herself all the suffering which life can lavish on a single soul."

This is one of those violent convictions and conclusions of which I spoke earlier, and it may be that it is for the families, the friends, the editors of those who want to learn how to write and sell short stories even more than for those who so yearn and strive—or should yearn and strive.

I do not believe movie stars are just like the little girl next door. If they are, I do not wish to see their pictures. For in ninety-nine cases out of a hundred the little girl next door is inarticulate and incapable of expressing herself or telling us what she is all about as Leslie Caron can. Grace Kelly can make you see her as the woman next door as the woman next door couldn't possibly, but Grace Kelly is not just like the woman next door! Doggoned if she is.

I do not believe those who can write short stories and have them read by millions are just like the people who deliver the laundry or sit behind typewriters in offices or sell you life insurance or doughnuts or even take care of you when you are sick. To my mind the most important job in the world is teaching, I know myself to be a frustrated schoolteacher, but I am not just like a schoolteacher or I would have been one and not fought my way to be a short story writer. I do not say short story writers—any kinds of storytellers—are better or greater or more important or worth while. I do say they are different, that they have been given a sensitive and peculiar gift, and that while some of them may have the gigantic soul strength and gusto and vitality and love of Ernest Hemingway, a lot of them don't.

There are too many examples of those who don't for anyone to question it. The sad story of that born storyteller, F. Scott Fitzgerald, is too well known to need repeating. Very plainly, living those stories to the full, being such a part of his times and then writing about them with such a glorious outflow of full emotion, compassion, pain, and panic as he saw the steam roller bearing down on him, surely this burned him up at forty-four. Long before that another great short story writer named Edgar Allan Poe, a pioneer of the American short story certainly, killed himself with his own "Fall of the House of Usher," the horror of his own "Rue Morgue" and "Gold Bug" and "Telltale Heart." The Reader's Encyclopedia, edited by William Rose Benét, however, says that his erratic temperament was "aggravated by poverty and unhappiness in his personal affairs," as, of course, whose isn't? Certainly that was also true of Stephen Crane, who, besides the *Red Badge of Courage*, wrote the unusual short story "The Open Boat" and died at twenty-nine. What storytellers those two young men were!

I am not trying to say that all good short story writers die young. They don't. Henry James lived to be seventy-three and was past fifty when he wrote the masterpiece called "The Turn of the Screw." The greatest of all, in my book, Rudyard Kipling, lived to be over seventy, as did Edith Wharton, whose immortal *Ethan Frome* is a bastard-length take that is as much a long short story as a short novel. Gilbert K. Chesterton, creator of Father Brown, had a life span of more than sixty years and Conan Doyle more than seventy. The present dean of short story writers, Somerset Maugham, is past eighty, and our beloved Mary Roberts Rinehart is approaching it.

What I would like to do is see that, if possible, none of them die young.

For all good short story writers—all storytellers—possess some degree of that artistic or erratic temperament which is composed of never failing sensitivity far beyond the average, or how could they see and feel so much more than others do? Of burning passion, of great warmth, of high voltage of all emotions. These can backfire, and yet they are absolutely essential, and to attempt to deny them, discredit them, overlook them is, I believe, the most dangerous process of all.

That creative temperament must be recognized as the gift of the gods—which it most definitely is—and safeguarded in every way possible.

Look at this historic example.

I quote from Louis Untermeyer's invaluable *A Treasury of Great Poems*: "One afternoon in his twenty-fifth year, he [Coleridge] took an opiate and fell asleep in a chair at the moment he was reading this sentence in Purchas' *Pilgrimage*: 'Here the Khan Kubla commanded a palace to be built, and a stately garden thereunto. And thus ten miles of fertile ground were enclosed with a wall.' Coleridge continued for about three hours in a profound sleep, and during that time he had, so he tells us, 'the most vivid confidence that he could not have composed less than from two to three hundred lines . . . without any sensation or consciousness of effort. On awaking, he appeared to himself to have a distant recollection of the whole, and taking his pen, ink, and paper, instantly and eagerly wrote down the lines that are here preserved. At this moment he was unfortunately called out by a person on business from Porlock and detained by him above an hour, and on return to his room found, to his no small surprise and mortification, that though he still retained some vague recollection of the general purport of the vision, yet with the exception of some eight or ten scattered lines and images, all the rest had passed away.' "

As Mr. Untermeyer comments, it is hard for lovers of poetry who recognize in what young Coleridge did put down of *Kubla Khan* a triumph of the imagination to forgive the person from Porlock.

Yet in a small way this can be done and is done daily by those who accept the increasingly accepted modern fallacy that artistic temperament is a lot of nonsense and ought to be suppressed at once. Once when I was a cub reporter covering the hotel beat and there interviewed the famous Canadian author, Sir Gilbert Parker, who wrote the short stories that made Pierre of the Plains a national hero, he said this to me, "As you go ahead with creative fiction, be very careful of your awakening moments in the morning. Train yourself to this. When you go to sleep at night, open your consciousness to the Source of imagination, and ask specifically for whatever you need or want in any story you are composing, or for a story itself in connection with something that has intrigued. Then, when you awaken, *do not open your eyes*. Lie quiet, with your eyes closed so that reality cannot impinge upon you, and very often you will find the full exposition of your story quite clear and definite in your mind."

At that time Sir Gilbert was an extremely dignified, bearded gentleman in his fifties, with a full quota of British reserve, the last man from whom temperament would have been expected.

I remember once during World War II going to call upon my idol, Mary Roberts Rinehart, who then lived just around the corner from me in New York and who was always pouring out the greatest and most gracious kindliness. Over a cup of tea, which we shared with my son, then a sergeant in Patton's Third Army, I asked her why she didn't please write some more stories about Tish, bringing her into this war as, say, an air raid warden. Mrs. Rinehart smiled at me, all pink and twinkly and so pretty, and said in a whisper, "Tish won't let me! She's been through so much, you know, she says she simply can't go through another war, and I really haven't been able to do anything about her. You know what Tish is!"

A witty jest? Y-y-yesss. Then again, No. No, no! That exquisite lady of high intelligence and social and professional prestige sitting there in her stately drawing room on Park Avenue knew Tish—and Aggie—surely Aggie—as well or better than she knew any real people.

Do people who aren't storytellers keep company with people who aren't real? My granddaughter Kristie once knew a small white dog named Bitsy. On occasions I was somewhat embarrassed when in a gas station she would insist that I get out and get Bitsy back into the car, where my own large German shepherd Ali watched the proceedings with a curious eye. I could see Ali all right but, try as I would, I was never able to see Bitsy and neither, of course, was the gas station attendant, who always looked a little green around the gills when Kristie said, "All right, Grammy, I have her now." But Kristie was five at the time. To keep this magic entry into another world after five is part of the artistic temperament.

Kipling saw the children in They—I know he did.

For when I met him crossing the English Channel, he agreed that of course Mowgli of *The Jungle Book*, and Bagheera the black panther and Kaa and Grey Brother were real. Realer than anybody, he agreed.

At that time I was several years past five and, crossing the Channel in a small boat on a very rough passage, I had blithely escaped from my aunt and uncle, who were being very unhappy and quite laid by the heels and, I think, didn't really care whether I—and they—all went to the bottom. The waves were breaking high, and as I staggered around the deck making up super sea stories of which I was the brave and dashing heroine, I thought I had the place to myself, except for an occasional sailor, until I barged into an old gentleman—he seemed old to me at the time—wrapped to his nose in a heavy coat, with a cap pulled down so that all I could see were a pair of thick glasses and a heavy mustache.

He held me upright and somehow we linked arms and began to make the exciting struggle around the slippery washing deck hanging on to each other, and in spite of the noise and everything else managed to hold quite a conversation. He knew—I couldn't imagine how—that I was an American, he said he liked America very much, his wife was an American, he said, and he asked me what I liked best to read and I told him, quite truthfully, *The Jungle Book*—I even, the ham in me of course, quoted to him the first few paragraphs, for I knew the whole book by heart at that point (still do most of it), to convince him that it was the best book ever written and next to it, I said, *A Midsummer Night's Dream.*

I asked him, stranger to me as he was, if he didn't feel that Mowgli was real. Realer than anybody, I said. He said, Oh yes, he knew Mowgli was real—and yes, Bagheera, who was my favorite. I would rather have met Bagheera then the King of England. Much rather. We talked all the way through the storm and the foul crossing about Mowgli and his friends, and then we landed, and in rejoining my poor limp relatives I lost sight of my friend, though he had asked me to write down my name and to tell him the name of the hotel where we were staying which I had done.

A few days later I received a copy of *The Jungle Book,* and written on the flyleaf were words that thrilled me a great deal more than most I have read since. Somewhere, I bitterly regret to say, in my many moves and among packing and unpacking my books, this one I treasured most was lost. But I remember the words perfectly. *To my little American friend, who knows that Mowgli is real as well as does the man who made him, Rudyard Kipling.*

How I wept because I had not known who he was, so that I could ask him questions, which probably was why he hadn't told me.

Without creative temperament, nobody makes Mowgli or Tish.

Two-edged sword, as we have seen. But it has to be part of how to write a short story and how to sell it, too. For, as we now know, they are one and the same. I feel that it is a part that is too often overlooked, too often dismissed. Instead of being developed, fed, encouraged, it is smothered. The cooking will be pretty doggone flat without it, my friends. It should be—*must be*—encouraged, though it has become the fashion to belittle it, to insist that it isn't necessary.

I never met Stephen Vincent Benét, I am sorry to say. He was, so everyone says who did know him, a Christlike man, of strength and humor and beauty of character, a creator. Certainly he possessed genius. Suppose when he, in that creative moment—that tune-in-to-the-Source—that spell of the imagination—that inspiration by the Muses or whatever it is—when "The Devil and Daniel Webster" was just coming into focus, suppose he had been jarred back to the everyday world by a person from Porlock or the telephone company, or even an editor or his family? I'm sure he never was, but it doesn't bear thinking about, and perhaps other stories as good have been murdered at conception by stupidity and carelessness and the fashion of the time.

A thoroughbred race horse can carry just so much weight and no more.

The artistic creative temperament can swim upstream just so far and hard—and no more.

This is one of the reasons we do not have as many good writers as we used to have, and the demand for stories comes from every direction.

Have temperament if you want to know how to write and

sell short stories. Have it, use it, foster it, tune in to it. Dive head first. Rejoice and sing. Skip among the hills and dance in the meadows and, having absorbed and loved and hated and lived and suffered today in this world, tomorrow begin to remold it nearer to the heart's desire.

Let me say here that I have never in my life known a short story writer who was any good at all who wasn't temperamental. It's impossible. It may be that fairy enchantment of Mary Roberts Rinehart's. Or the simple, endearing Hiram Holiday quality of Paul Gallico. Or the distinguished touchy brilliance of Edna Ferber. Or the strange where-am-I vagueness of William Faulkner.

You think Willa Cather, the author of "Paul's Case" and "Coming, Aphrodite," wasn't temperamental? Read the late books about Willa and how she worked by her friends who lived with her during her most creative years.

I find that I have many violent conclusions about all this which I did not know about before. (My children have never quite forgiven the fellow who beat them to the title My Mother Is a Violent Woman.) I have a reverence for my own profession which is far beyond what I had realized. I didn't know I had learned as much about how to write a short story as I have; the exploratory journey is leading to much that I didn't know I had absorbed and recognized by experience and trial and error and heartache and that something inside that makes you write and a close and constant study of my betters. I find I want very much to put it all down for anyone else who wants to write short stories, really wants to, has to, can't bear not to. So much of it is not mine, I find. I have had it hammered into my thick skull and through my thin skin, and in spite of my touchy pride and easily broken heart, by great editors like above all Herbert Mayes, and then Ray Long and Jack O'Connell and William Frederick Bigelow and Graeme Lorimer and Frances Whiting and James R. Quirk and Sumner Blossom and Kenneth Littauer and Stuart Rose and Bruce Gould and Geraldine Rhoads and Eleanor Stierhem Rawson and Bill Nichols.

All this has really happened to me.

What I know, I *know*. The sleepless nights are my own. None of what came of it is great, though I believe I have written two good short stories, and that's not bad, as you will see, and I'm still hopeful. And none of it is unpublished.

There is always room at the top, and this is true.

I would still rather be a newspaper reporter than anything else in the world but I am too old in the legs now for that young man's game, and I find that translating it all into short stories is the thing I like to do now more than anything else.

Now we're going to get down to the hard work and the sweat and the things that are absolutely vital if a writer is to be read. I can say that those who can make the grade and become professional, producing short story writers are the luckiest men and women, boys and girls, on earth anywhere, as Paul Gallico and I decided for an entire day recently when we were crossing a lot of desert between Phoenix and Las Vegas in his English Rolls-Bentley and were about to be most royally entertained at the Flamingo Hotel while he picked up some articles for the *Reader's Digest* and I got two short stories.

It's worth trying, learning, working, suffering, and praying for—and that I tell you for sure.

Now.

The next thing is—what is a short story and how do you know one when you meet it?

5. A short story is a story that can be adequately and even superbly told *short*.

Webster says a story is a tale, especially a fictitious narrative less elaborate than a novel.

He also adds that it may be a fib, a lie, a falsehood, and that "told a story" is a euphemism used chiefly by or to children. This is also true, and I well remember my first attempts at storytelling to entertain my neighbors. I went from door to door and told everybody in the block that my mother had twin boys and that they were on the screen porch in the washtub. The germ of this tale is easy to trace, for I wanted somebody in the family to have twin boys and my imagination swiftly leaped the gap between the dull reality that nobody *had* and the blissful state which I could so well visualize of the twins on the screen porch in the washtub. Their names, I recall distinctly, were Hans (from Hans Brinker, I assume) and Bottom.

Naturally this got back to my folks, as callers began to arrive, somewhat dubious since there had been no previous indication of twins being about to arrive in the Rogers household. My father received them with what grace he could, saved my face to the best of his ability, and then took the matter up with me personally.

In a collection of my short stories called *Never Again and Other Stories* I told it this way, and I can't seem to better it at the moment:

"Telling tales, tall and otherwise, was born in me.

"Somewhere around 1903–4–5 there was a conviction in the neighborhood where I lived that 'the little Rogers girl' was the biggest liar since Baron Münchausen. At first this hurt and bewildered me, and finally after pulling a couple of boys off their bicycles and trying to settle the issue with bare knuckles and a bit of hair-pulling, I went to my father.

"Between us, we worked out to my satisfaction the difference between a story and a lie.

"My dad explained to me that a lie was a deliberate betrayal of Truth. It was to mislead my listeners as to facts and people, or to state a falsity when I was asked point-blank what happened.

"A story, on the other hand, he told me, was something I manufactured out of the glorious material given me by my imagination. My father called imagination the Gateway to Reality. He said that often a story was something I wished to be true, and quoted to me from Omar about remolding things nearer to my heart's desire. It was sailing the perilous seas of fairyland forlorn. Or, he said, it was passing something which had actually happened through the spectrum of my imagination so that the hearer could see the points of reality and beauty which Nature had intended without seeing the signboards humanity had put up in front of them.

"As long, he said, as I labeled my story—any story—I had a right, even a duty, to tell it. And he would show me how that had been done by others in the past. Shakespeare, for instance, in A Midsummer Night's Dream—for which I thank him daily—for I grew up without that horror of the marble bust called Shakespeare with which so many children are cursed.

"All that was pretty wonderful, as I look back on it, and I became a sort of pre-radio minstrel to the neighborhood kids, and have been making my living that way ever since."

My grandfather, a college president and Methodist minister, was also called in, and he persuaded me, encouraged me, and helped me to begin to write my tales down on paper. One of his, about the first watermelons he ever took to market and what happened, was the one I wrote down in a large childish scrawl and sold for a dollar to the Los Angeles Times. My first earned buck. They tell me I have earned a fantastic number since by the same method and I am very grateful.

I didn't, then, realize how lucky I was. I suppose I thought all little girls and boys had fathers and grandfathers who knew the difference between lying and storytelling and could set a child's feet on the right path. I have learned since, for I have seen the lovely gift beaten out of youngsters by stupid, narrow, nervous parents and teachers, when all that was needed was what my father and grandfather did for me.

So, according to the dictionary, a short story would be a short tale, especially a short fictitious narrative less elaborate than a novel.

As I said in the beginning of this chapter, a short story is a story that can be adequately told short.

There are no other rules.

Absolutely none.

Today the short means anywhere from three thousand to seven thousand words, preferably four to five thousand.

This does not include short shorts, which I am too old a dog to learn the new trick of, and there is an excellent book about it by the editor of *This Week* which includes a number of fine examples of the type.

When I say there are no rules about short stories, I make one exception. The rule is they should be good. Rich. Filled with temperament and desire to tell them.

Otherwise the story may be about anything.

Any kind of people young or old, black, white, brown or yellow, good or bad, rich or poor, short or tall, lean or fat, funny or solemn, pagans or true believers, sick or well, smart or stupid, poets or peasants, dogs or cats.

As long as they are people the writer knows.

The story may cover centuries or minutes. Continents and the air above them and the water underneath and even trips to the moon, though I don't recommend any more of those right now. Or it may take place on a park bench.

It may be told in the first or third person, and as to grammar, it has to some degree ceased to exist if the story is best told by ignoring the rules of grammar to give it reality and flavor, as witness Runyon and Lardner and often Sherwood Anderson. What rules there are about that seem to me included in Fowler's *Modern English Usage*, which Maugham so highly recommends and from which I am never separated. This man wrote about grammar for the particular problems of writers.

Adventure. Science Fiction. Love. Teen-Age. Lavender and Old Lace. New Yorker. Mood. Detective. Ghost. Character. War. Religious.

These at least are a few of the kinds of short stories there are.

With a thousand thousand variations therefrom.

They may bring tears, laughter, furious indignation, curiosity—as long as they bring something to the reader.

There is only one thing they must possess. One quality that must be common to them all. Whether they are as serious as Theodore Dreiser or as amusing as James Thurber. One factor without which no art can make them succeed:

Entertainment.

James Farley, the greatest campaign manager of all time, once told me that there was only one quality a candidate for office must have. He must be electable.

A short story must be readable.

Willy-nilly whether or not, it must entertain.

6. To illustrate the last chapter:

The master of short stories is Rudyard Kipling.

Let us study for a moment the range of his interest, the warmth of his response to life, the depth, breadth, width, and height of his feeling about everything he saw or heard.

The vital quality to be cultivated by anyone who wants to know how to write short stories is reaction. Constant and never failing interest.

Your required reading at this point is the following Kipling stories after you have become aware of the utterly amazing facts about them. For here, plain and proven, are to be seen stories by Rudyard Kipling in every possible field—and they are all the best of their kind. I remember an evening in my home in Cow Lane, Great Neck, when a group had gathered which included, as I recall it now, Clarence Budington Kelland, Paul Gallico, Frances Whiting, Damon Runyon, Katharine Brush, and a number of very good illustrators and artists such as John LaGatta, Jack Sheridan, and E.M. Jackson. We decided to discover what we thought was the best short story ever written, and so that there wouldn't be influence—Bud Kelland can always influence anybody to practically anything and I am sure I wouldn't have dared to go against any conclusion of his—we would write out our selections and put them in a hat. I've forgotten the exact stories, but all except one were by Kipling. More than that, in the discussion that followed, we all agreed that as writers we had learned more, been more inspired to go and do likewise by a careful and joyous study of his short stories than by anything else that had ever happened to us except work, which is the hard way and can to some small extent be lightened by those who have gone before us on the same path. As you know, a couple of years ago Somerset Maugham edited an exciting one-volume collection of Kipling short stories, which shows what he thinks about Mr. Kipling, because Somerset Maugham undoubtedly knows more about short story writing than anyone else in the world today, and he hasn't edited a collection of anybody else's short stories.

One way, perhaps the best way, to definition is the show one. This, I inform my granddaughter Kathleen (age one year) as I point to the picture, is a CAT. She believes me. After a while when I turn to that picture she beats me to it. CAT, she says. Then comes the glorious day when she sees my Grey Brother walking across the lawn and with a great light bursting on her face she yells CAT. This can happen about short stories, too. Suddenly one day as you look at something or somebody you will shout SHORT STORY. That is the way it happened to my blessed April Oursler, Fulton Oursler's daughter, whose *Fátima: Pilgrimage to Peace* I hope you have read, but I propose to devote a whole chapter to that. Anyhow, I am reminded that the first step between us, which led eventually to a short story written, sold, and read, was a corking row about Kipling's short stories, which, having been but recently graduated from a ladies' college, she regarded as crude. Later she reversed that opinion of course, being both highly gifted and of a fair and open mind.

These then are short stories, taken by Mr. Kipling, as you will see, from anything and everything that life can offer.

"The Brushwood Boy" is a warm, delicate young love story. Note the way he uses dreams as the device for his desire to tell you that two people were born and intended for each other from the beginning. "Don't you remember the Thirty-Mile-Ride with me—when They were after us—on the beach-road, with the sea on the left—going towards the lamp-posts on the downs?" Georgie asked Miss Lacy. She remembered. He makes you believe it. And the Lily Lock beyond Hong-Kong and Java.

"Krishna Mulvaney" is many things, but it is beyond anything else the full-blooded creation of a character. Mulvaney walks off the paper all right, and into your life for as long as that life lasts—and maybe a little longer.

"Bimi" is the best horror story I know, unless it might be "The End of the Passage," which Mr. Kipling also wrote, and of course "The Phantom Rickshaw" has few superiors as a ghost story.

"The Devil and the Deep Sea" is called by Paul Gallico "that epic of man against machinery," and he further says of it, in his *Confessions of a Story Writer*, " 'McKabe,' the first fiction story I sold to *The Saturday Evening Post*, was made up of a kind of hero worship I had long entertained for the working newspaperman, the killing of a notorious gangster, and the urge to imitate a short story by Rudyard Kipling called 'The Devil and the Deep Sea.' "

It is profitable to stop here and note that Mr. Gallico has given us a perfect recipe for a good short story, which "McKabe" is. One third hero worship, or strong emotion. One third from life, the killing of Legs Diamond. One third method, how to put it on paper, that urge to imitate a specific story by Kipling. Two thirds, you see, is emotion—urge—desire. Observe also please that all these things were and are available to anybody anywhere anytime. Hero worship is possible to anyone who has a soul for it, and if he hasn't he shouldn't try to be a short story writer. The Legs Diamond murder was on the front pages and there's hardly a day when it isn't. That epic of man against machinery, "The Devil and the Deep Sea," is in every library free, for nothing.

All it takes after that is reaction. Response. Recognition. Susceptibility to drama. Keeping the soul and heart and mind and eyes and ears wide open all the time. All the time.

"Wee Willie Winkie" is a great child story. How good

stories become part of a family, of people's lives. My oldest son was 6.3 by the time he went to high school, and since his name was William, it was only natural that we called him Wee Willie. When his son came along he had to be Winkie, didn't he? He was, for years, though now that he's going to college this fall he winces when he hears the name, so even Grammy has learned to call him Bill. We also as a family are devoted to the lemmings, not, I have to admit, because of John Masefield's sonnet but on account of James Thurber's fable, and a fable is a short story and all fables are very good springboards for modern short stories, too.

Right up at the top of animal stories must come "Rikki-Tikki-Tavi," about a mongoose, and "Toomai of the Elephants." I am playing scrupulously fair in not mentioning *The Jungle Book*. Those are not really short stories even on the basis of a series; you must know Mowgli from the moment he comes up the hill to Mother Wolf's cave. A short story, even in a series, must always be complete for the reader who has never met any of the characters before.

"Love-o-Women" is a good murder, "A Second-Rate Woman" is a sophisticated Maugham type, for sheer comedy there is "An Unsavory Interlude" from a series called *Stalky and Company*, for science fiction there is "The Bridge-Builders," and for a religious gem "The Gardener." One of the greatest sob or human interest tales ever written is "Without Benefit of Clergy," which is also a terrific love story, and I know no more moving and engrossing fantasy than "Wireless."

"The Maltese Cat" is as good a sports story as anybody has written up to now. When *Sports Illustrated* was starting, I made what I still think was a bright suggestion, which was that they reprint the classic sports fiction stories, most of which by the sheer nature of things have not been known to this present generation of readers, just as the movies remake and reissue for their new audiences every ten years. I would have started with the best of all race track stories, "The Look of Eagles," gone on to R. G. Kirk's "Glenmere White Monarch and the Gas House Pup" and then "The Maltese Cat"— who was, of course, a polo pony, perfect player of The Game. But sadly for those who will miss these and a golf story by Charlie Van Loan and the baseball classic by Ring Lardner, "Alibi Ike," and a Lucian Cary story called, I think, "Tennis Bum," and of course Jack London's fight masterpiece, "A Piece of Steak" and—anyhow, the editor of *Sports Illustrated* didn't think it was a good idea and he certainly knows more about his own magazine than I do. I had fun thinking about it, though. And rereading the stories myself.

Now you must be conscious of the incredible range of subjects and people that made short stories for the master, Rudyard Kipling. If you will read them with care you should feel like a Little Leaguer who has watched Al Kaline or Mickey Mantle all season, or a violin student who has seen and heard Heifetz, or a young scientist who lived next door to Einstein.

This, you will say to yourself, is how short stories are written.

Two vital points appear beside the deep spiritual faith in the short story as a means of entertainment and communication and enlightenment, and man's ability to write them.

Kipling always had a story to tell.

But it was hardly ever a very new story. He didn't strive for the unusual in plot or approach or even background.

He had a story he wanted to tell and it became a story because of that great desire, that passionate urge. He wanted to tell it, and it poured out of him with fervor and excitement, with a completely unegotistical conviction that this was a great story and therefore must be told and he was the channel, the vessel, the mouthpiece, the amanuensis.

He found stories everywhere. Nothing escaped him. Nobody escaped him, he was undoubtedly a born storyteller, and there must be some of that or it is hardly worth while for anyone to try this profession. Kipling was never afraid of a story because it was too big or too little, too old or too new, he picked ideas up any time, anyhow, from anybody. He was, I can testify, a listener, not a talker, and that is true of most good short story writers. They listen. It is amazing what stories about and on themselves people will tell, in beauty parlors, in cocktail lounges, on trains, in cars or hotel lobbies or department stores or over coffee cups. Kipling, as his stories prove, listened on street corners, aboard tramp steamers, in barracks, at dinner parties, in hot city rooms. He remembered from his childhood, his school days, his young manhood. His hero worship led him to watch bridges being built and railroad engines being run and doctors and civil servants living their own lives all around him. He had as many eyes as a peacock and ears as long as a donkey's and a memory like a tape recorder.

He knew what a story was.

It was something that happened to people.

Something moving or dangerous or exciting or terrible or heartbreaking or unusual or usual or glorious or triumphant.

But whatever it was that happened and no matter how many thousand times a man and a girl had lived together without benefit of clergy, it was always a story and always different if it happened to different people—to somebody who was real, so that as the reader forgot his own life and world he lived for a time with a man named Holden and a girl named Ameera, who said, "Look at the child, love of my life, he is counting stars too."

Everything was a potential story to Kipling.

That must be implanted deep and firm in the mind of the man or woman, girl or boy who wants to write short stories. Look for stories everywhere. Somerset Maugham says that if he spent an hour with any person he would be able to write some kind of story about that person, and I would guarantee to do the same. We couldn't have done it of course in the beginning, but we learned by always looking, watching, expecting, listening for stories.

A few minutes ago I looked out my big window. It framed a picture. A tall, slim, very pretty girl in delicious and fashionable summer resort shorts and shirt, her hair burnished in the sunshine, and a rugged, good-looking young man in Levi's and a torn white sweat shirt were leaning on the tail gate of a moving van, completely absorbed in each other's conversation. I had seen the truck arrive and back up to the little hotel cottage under the orange trees and the big tanned truck driver carry out some elegant luggage, and now I could also see Mama, pretty and dainty in a little figured summer dress, fluttering as she peered out her window.

There has to be a story there, doesn't there? Surely I have something to say about that?

The wonderful ideas Herbert Mayes of *Good Housekeeping* has given me through the years have often been only a sentence or two—but always they have been stories. Usually in the form of questions.

What is the longest walk in the world? And when I, as an old police reporter said, To the electric chair, Herb said, Oh no, from the head of the aisle to the altar.

What happens to a woman very much in love with her husband when he goes to jail for ten years?

Mr. Mayes asked me that one day in his office, looking at me with the delicate smile of a Borgia—in appearance our Mr. Mayes is a combination of Caesar, of that ilk, and the young St. Sebastian and, come to think of it, so are his character and disposition—and instantly it went together with a woman I'd long admired because she was so lustily, honestly, and magnificently in love with her husband, a thing so few women seem able to achieve, and I thought, Poor thing, she'd be neither maid, wife nor widow—which turned out to be the title of the story.

Again the progression is exciting. Mr. Mayes got the thought for his question from the story then in the newspapers of a man of wealth and social position who had been sentenced to a ten-year term in Sing Sing. To it, I added this woman I had been watching for months, listening to for years, and then it took me three or four months to get an ending. During those months I wasn't fit to live with, I suppose, because there was never a moment when I wasn't trying to find it. I kept looking at people to see if they had it hidden and I prayed about it every night and kept my eyes closed every morning, and then one day I got on a train and went up to Sing Sing and there it was! As soon as I saw the walls, there it was. Love is, if it be true love, a spiritual thing and can leap over walls and melt them down. I knew that. I wanted to say it.

What does a man do who used to pray but has lost faith when something terrible that only prayer could help happens to him?

You see, Mr. Mayes' genius lies not in giving you a plot, or an idea, but in the great impulse and urge that he arouses in you to answer his questions fully in fiction form. I have learned how to make up questions myself and you can too, but they aren't as good, naturally.

Out of that one came the story I like best of all the things I have written. "The First Morning," it is called, and it appeared in *Good Housekeeping*. If a story of mine were to be included in this book, "The First Morning" is the one I would choose.

It took longer to complete than any of the others.

In fact, it was almost a year before I started to write it.

I had the question and I knew the answer. In about a month I had the man complete, I knew him intimately, I'd campaigned with him. This time the story had to be right and I didn't have it. It had to be something quick and vital that would of itself say everything I wanted to say of suspense and terror, of something that only prayer could do anything about. Like war, like a son at war, but it mustn't be war, that was too special. This had to be something that could happen to anybody any day. So I put it in the hopper, or the reservoir, and tied it to the Source as best I could, and waited. I prayed a good deal myself.

One morning I woke up, wide awake, and fully conscious, saying to myself, "I know. The time Ken went up the hills back of Azusa when the kid fell off the cliff." Ken Dare is my son-in-law, a very fine newspaper photographer. So I picked up the phone and called him and a startled voice said in one of those emergency tones, "What is it?" and I looked at the clock and it was ten minutes to four. So I hung up without saying anything, rose, made coffee, and paced the floor in a state of exaltation and glory until it was light, then I drove across the canyon to the Valley and had breakfast with Ken and got him to tell me in great detail about climbing up the cliffs with the forest rangers to see if the bundle of clothes at the foot was the missing boy—and it was.

Then I tried to make the boy's father, who in my story went up with them, come off the paper and be as real to the reader as he was to me, so that when he did pray, they prayed with him.

I think they did because I had numerous letters telling me that they did and even some prayer groups and cells used the story as an example.

You must be prepared to spend your life looking for stories.

Above all things, start where you are.

It may be years before you can go traveling around the world, as Maugham has done, as Gallico does.

But Damon Runyon never traveled more than a couple of blocks each way on Broadway and maybe up to Boston once in a while.

Years ago Mary E. Wilkins Freeman wrote a story I've never forgotten—I imagine it is in her collection called *A Humble Romance*—about a woman whose husband kept building bigger and bigger barns but wouldn't build her a new house, so one day he came in from the south forty and found she had moved out to the barn. All the furniture and everything.

Go back and read Sherwood Anderson's *Winesburg, Ohio.*

Or Scott Fitzgerald's early short stories around the people he knew.

Or Alfred Henry Lewis' Wolfville tales.

Or Booth Tarkington's *Penrod.*

Or James Thurber's "The Secret Life of Walter Mitty."

Or Mark Twain's "The Celebrated Jumping Frog of Calaveras County."

Or Dorothy Parker's "Big Blonde."

Or Huxley's "The Gioconda Smile."

Or Robert Louis Stevenson's "A Lodging for a Night."

You don't have to go anywhere to write any of those.

They were written, as were Kipling's first stories—those *Plain Tales from the Hills* that made him almost instantaneously famous—right where the writer was. Stevenson was in bed—a hopeless invalid. And he became entranced with a figure who had lived a couple of hundred years before he did. Big blondes are everywhere. So are Gioconda smiles. And Penrods! You can't hardly go anyplace no more without finding Penrods.

The title of *Plain Tales* is an accurate one.

They are plain tales. Ordinary tales. But they are stories.

This is the first essential thing. Begin to look all around all the time for stories.

Ninety-two per cent of the time, the elapsed time, on a short story is, with a few rare exceptions, spent before you put pencil or typewriter to paper.

7.

Paul Gallico and I were dining one evening at Romanoff's, where we go not because it is the most famous restaurant in Beverly Hills but because we are devoted to its host, Mike Romanoff.

Over some delicious chicken which Paul had ordered—he is a gourmet and a connoisseur of food and I once heard him and Marcia Davenport wax lyrical for some time over a certain kind of mushroom to be found only in the Tyrolean Alps and a Chinese café on Mott Street—we listened to Mike tell a tale of a small midwestern town where he once spent a weekend. Quarter of the way through, Gallico and I were avoiding each other's eyes. Halfway, we had glanced coldly at each other. When Mike had presented the touching and satisfactory climax, our eyes met and I said bitterly, "All right. It's yours. It's your kind of a story, not mine."

During our stay in Las Vegas, they finally exploded a long-awaited atomic bomb. We stayed up all night to see it and at five in the morning found ourselves outside the Flamingo Hotel with Gwen and Ray Bolger staring at the distant sky, which for one swift, incredible moment had gone all light, green-white light, and then showed only a strange fussy gray mushroom. I glanced at Gallico and knew our faces mirrored each other, though his is large and darkly Italianate and picturesquely masculine and mine has the map of Ireland on it and is, I like to think, kind and grandmotherly, though at times the effect seems to be otherwise. But the expressions were the same. You get an idea? Ought to be some kind of a story in any atomic bomb blast. Well, keep thinking about it and one will come. Mine did, a couple of weeks later. I've forgotten to ask Paul, who has retired once more to his alp and writes from there, "Because of traveling I was slower getting into production than you on the material we picked up together. But now I have sold the first to the *Post*, 'The Silent Hostages'; you remember the one about the two killers who blunder into Doomtown and stick up a couple of dummies. It wasn't easy, but it came off."

This is to give you a brief glimpse of a couple of old pros at work.

We talked shop, which means stories, for weeks and miles.

I doubt if there ever was a moment when that deep important layer of sensitive sponge just under the surface of social chat wasn't actively absorbing, sorting, selecting, rejecting, retaining impressions. Putting them away sometimes in bits and pieces, sometimes laying one out all but an end or beginning, once in a while getting one whole.

Maybe someday that good-looking young man rolling dice

with such an expert hand, and quite, quite silently, will come in handy. Maybe the pretty waitress in a lunchroom down near the railroad tracks in Needles who looked as though she belonged in 21 instead will play a part. Maybe the teen-age girl who looked at Gallico's Rolls-Bentley with bright dark eyes and said to the redheaded boy, "It don't look much fun to me, I'd rather have ours," will put a topper on something.

I am trying to find a way to tell you how to recognize a story. How to know what a story is.

For I believe that is the thing most people who want to write short stories need to know and don't know.

Why?

On the whole I think it is because they are always looking for something outside themselves, something distant, something stupendous and dramatic, taking place if possible in Paris, where they have never been, or the South Seas, ditto, or having to do with something of vast significance which they know nothing about at all.

I am inclined to say here that anyone who has no story sense, who hasn't at least a few ideas and responses and reactions ought to find some other profession. When I run into a writer who isn't working because he hasn't any ideas, or is waiting for a story, I know that he isn't a real storyteller.

At a time when I lived in Great Neck, Long Island, I had the privilege of Bud Kelland's friendship and the delight of frequent visits from him, usually after a golf game when the others had gone to the nineteenth hole, which sometimes bored Bud. So he would come by my house of happy memory in Cow Lane and talk story. His trouble always was a positive fury—and the great Clarence Budington Kelland is a furious man—that he had so many stories he wanted to tell, had to tell, that he'd never live long enough to write 'em all if he got to be a hundred and fifty, which I hope he does. He would sit there looking like a pixie made of the best walnut, his bright bright blue eyes sparkling, and sputter with his famous wit about his sad plight.

Stories are things that happen to people.

Or to you and people.

Sometimes of course they are hurricanes and earthquakes and wars, but let me reiterate that they are better stories if they happen to people.

Mostly they are not hurricanes and earthquakes and wars.

If you look, you are apt to find one right beside you. Or hear one tonight when you go over to watch the ball game on television with your neighbors. Or on the counter at the corner drugstore at lunch time.

Most stories begin with people.

Some with what I suppose should be called a theme, though I don't like the word, but it seems the one best understood in this connection.

Some with a strange incident or happening, or offbeat or unusual circumstance or situation in which people do or could find themselves.

A few years ago a brilliant young editor named Geraldine

Rhoads, who was then on a really good magazine that folded because it couldn't get a sufficient number of good short stories to sustain its program and is now with *Reader's Digest*, said to me, "The thing I want most is some short stories about young married couples. Their present-day problems."

I said, "Well, my young married days are a long way behind me, this I tell you for sure. But there must be a lot of young writers who could do those stories. I had half a dozen in my classes at UCLA who had matrimonial problems that everybody on the campus knew about."

"Yes," Gerry said, "but they won't write about them. They will not recognize them as stories. They will not look close at hand. One of the best of them has just sent me a story about a girl who knew the man who shot Lincoln. It's not very good because she doesn't know enough yet to make a story and people she's had no personal contact with, a background she never saw, come to life."

Later in the conversation I got to telling Gerry and a girl who became fiction editor of *Collier's*, Eleanor Stierhem Rawson, about a political campaign my son Mac had handled, and in the midst of it they looked at each other and said, "How about that?" So I did them, two long short stories called "The Candidate's Wife," and "The Congressman's Wife," which their young married readers liked, so I guess they were accurate reporting of young married life today. But it still does not seem that I, at sixty, should be stealing all the terrific stories in that field, which is full of young writers.

I am lucky, of course, to have editors who pick stories out of our conversations, which is their business and mine.

That was the peculiar and unique gift of Frances Whiting, who as an editor was a great favorite with all writers including Sinclair Lewis, a hard man to get along with because he was so temperamental and shy. I loved la belle Whiting for herself I hope, but I am honest enough to admit that from the day she made Burton buy "Never Again" and I had my first conversation with her I found her invaluable to talk to. We had lunched together one day at the Plaza and had sat happily looking out over the park and, as far as I was concerned, paying little attention to business, which in her case was to edit *Cosmopolitan* and in mine to write short stories for it. At that time I had a house in Beekman Place on the river, with a lot of bedrooms which my own sons weren't occupying, being otherwise occupied in the armed forces. I was glad through the Travelers Aid to offer them to other servicemen, and at lunch I had been telling Frances about some of the boys who had stayed there, particularly a corporal and his bride who had spent their wedding night with me. Late that afternoon I received a call from Miss Whiting, who said, "I'd like to have a short story about that corporal and his wife spending their wedding night in someone's New York house." We called it "Wedding Night," and it was a very popular tale. This was only one of half a dozen stories—"Unto Us," "Walking on Air," "Where One Grew Before"—which came out of talks between us; sometimes I heard them myself, sometimes Frances Whiting spotted something I didn't. An idea rings a bell inside you.

At first you will have to do this for yourself, do your own watching, listening, recognizing. But *do it*. Start where you are, with the people around you.

Let's take a fine example that everyone knows.

Mister Roberts.

In the beginning this was a series of short stories all laid on a ship and most of them around one character—Mister Roberts.

Tom Heggen, who wrote them, was a young sailor who was on such a ship during the war. I think Tom had the greatest writing talent—storytelling talent—of any young writer I've met. I had lunch with him in New York one day—and on the train going West heard of his death and I wept bitterly, partly for the charming, shy, awkward boy I'd grown so fond of and partly for the brilliant storyteller we'd lost. I was sure he was going on to Pulitzer and even Nobel prizes, that lad. Because on top of a great story mind, *he would work.* He loved working. He was utterly absorbed by stories all the time. He could learn things, too, he didn't know so much already that he couldn't be told something—even with his tremendous success.

His admiration for Sinclair Lewis was very great, and I told him one thing that Red had taught me. About names. Red couldn't write about characters unless the names fitted them in his consciousness. He told me it took him months to find Babbitt—which became part of our language, and Arrowsmith, and Dodsworth. He told me that he got halfway through a book one time and knew it was all wrong, nothing worked, the man was of straw, not flesh and blood, and then he discovered he had the wrong name for him. This is true, I think, of every writer. I search the telephone book, Burke's Peerage, the society sections of the Sunday papers, I keep a notebook and put down names I like—not unusual ones, necessarily. The ones I find in there at the moment are Shannon, Les, Valdez, Adrienne, Chess, Miss Billings, Thea, Rance, Alix, Coralie, and Hap. They don't seem to amount to much, but they may fit somebody. I believe Red Lewis was right and that you cannot create a character properly if the name isn't right in your own mind.

I told Tom Heggen, too, about a time when Red Lewis dropped into my Beekman Place house, white and cross because the book he was working on wouldn't come the way he wanted it to. I knew a little something of what he was doing and I took my courage in both hands and said, "Could it be because you are drawing the key character from life but for personal reasons are drawing away from it all the time so she won't be recognized? Sometimes that pulls everything out of shape." He gave me one of those strangely sweet almost fey looks that were so surprising and—somehow childlike—and left almost immediately. It wasn't, when it appeared, a very good book, but the best thing in it was the character of Winifred the Talking Woman and—some people thought they recognized her.

You have to be *ruthless*.

Mostly you are safe.

The truer to life you get the less likely people are to recognize themselves. So few of them have any idea of what they look like to others or what they actually are. I well remember a famous movie star from whom I had drawn a short story character none too savory saying to me, "I expect Gloria Swanson was furious with you!"

Tom Heggen in one of our long before-the-fire sessions told me that the stories of *Mister Roberts*, which have now been used successfully in every medium for telling stories this side of the moon—magazines, book, stage, radio, movies, and television—came just because he was so interested in the men on his ship—and other ships.

"That was all, really," he said. "I suppose they were just ordinary guys, actually, like all the men on all the other ships. That was why I—I was so interested in them. Most of us, writers and readers, are pretty ordinary too. So we—we meet each other in stories. Communicate. Everyone wants to communicate—they're lonesome. I'm lonesome myself, that's why I like to make up people, then you're never lonesome."

Tom was fascinated by the very ordinariness of the men on his ship and their reactions to ordinary situations intensified by the isolation and boredom of their part in the war. The men in *Mister Roberts* could be, and were and are, the men working next to you in a factory, or a shoe shop, or a law office. The intensification of their characters came from boredom, and

The Captain was The Boss. Men get bored in factories, too, or stores, or law offices.

In his *Biographia Literaria*, Coleridge explains the schedule he and Wordsworth had worked out to produce *Lyrical Ballads*. They were to show the two basic roots from which any creative writing stems, and the two powers which it always has. "The power of exciting the sympathy of the reader by a faithful adherence to the truth of nature, and the power of giving the interest of novelty to the modifying colors of imagination." So Coleridge puts it, and further says that Wordsworth was to take subjects from ordinary life: "The characters and incidents were to be such as will be found in every village and vicinity." He himself was to take persons and characters "supernatural, or at least romantic; yet so as to procure for these shadows of imagination that willing suspension of disbelief for the moment which constitutes poetic faith."

That great poet, those great poets, for they shared their work and beliefs, were concerned to excite the sympathy of the reader, so they intended their poetry to be read, and they wanted to make their characters so real that the reader would have faith in them, whether the characters came from everyday life or from imagination. Wordsworth's were to come from life, from every small town, every place he happened to be, city or countryside.

Perhaps I am belaboring a point here. But it is one that my experience insists needs belaboring. All of us who deal with aspiring writers grow a little weary of having them say, "But *that* isn't a story," when events in or around their own village or vicinity are mentioned in spite of the proof that the majority of successful writers have always used them.

Plain tales are all around you. Always.

I remember one day watching Harlan Ware's face as a lady from down the street aways burst into praise of his daughter Joy. Joy is now a settled and successful sophomore in college, but then she was a beloved but problem teen-ager and Harlan and his incomparable wife Ruth (that is one of the trials of being a woman short story writer: you cannot have a wife like Ruth Ware or John Reese's Maggie, and how a short story writer needs one you will know only when you become a short story writer)—anyway, Harlan and Ruth had just been through one of those teen-age crises and Harlan was dumfounded to hear that his neighbor was saying, "We do think Joy is the dearest girl we know and her manners are charming, so different from Diane's," and then she added bitterly, "Sometimes I think I'll end by throttling Diane."

"But," Harlan said in a faraway voice, "we've always thought Diane was such a comfort to you . . ."

I beheld the glint in his eye as the sentence faded.

Sure enough.

He made of it an enchanting short story about what two fathers who were next-door neighbors thought and did about each other's sons, sold it to *Collier's,* where it was published and brought delight and enlightenment to many readers. I admit it had all the slightly offbeat, pixilated charm that distinguishes Ware's short stories, a difficult thing to achieve without going all over whimsical, but the idea was certainly open to every writer, for few of us have not some connection with teen-agers.

My point is that there are story ideas everywhere that have heart and meaning and reader identification.

If you want to be a storyteller, start telling stories. To anybody who will listen. Or if nobody will or you are the kind who cannot talk them, go off and tell them to yourself. Tell them constantly in your head. Put them together in your own mind. Live with your characters until you can actually hold conversations with them. Your family will soon get used to it. They become part of it. Look what James Thurber did with his family. His grandfather is almost my favorite character in the whole world, and don't tell me anybody but Thurber was Grandpa just that way, either. You have to be utterly ruthless with your family.

So you start brooding.

Over a story idea.

Maybe it starts with:

A person. Your sister-in-law. Your boss. A girl you used to be in love with. A teacher you had in high school. Your best friend's husband. I don't know. I met an old lady the other day who lost the key to her safe deposit box and turned out the whole Redlands police department.

Or a theme. Maybe you are boiling about that story in the paper this morning about a half-baked deputy sheriff who shot a youngster when the boy ran away from a parole-violation pinch. Or—I'm boiling because the other night I heard a wife say to her husband in front of half a dozen people, "After all, dear, it's my money."

Or the odd circumstances of some friends of yours who rented a house and found the folks next door were Koreans, or the wife was obviously no better than she should be, or they left the baby home alone while they went down to the corner for a drink.

Which reminds me that Ring Lardner once made a fine story out of a bridge game—Ring spent a lot of time playing bridge. His is called "Who Dealt?" Get a copy of *Round Up*, the Lardner stories—and if you don't own one you should— and read it. If you can't learn something from that, you are beyond redemption.

Don't expect all ideas to come whole. Very, very, very few do. Once in a while one springs full-orbed from the head of Jove and you say Thank you to the Source of all creative processes. Jesse Stuart has this to say in Whit Burnett's rather dull and ponderous *This Is My Best* (authors so seldom know which, don't they?), "I knew every detail of this story ["Another April"] before I sat down to the typewriter. The story wrote itself. My mind was only a medium to put it on paper. This was one of Nature's own stories, that Nature and Life had worked out together."

This happened to me on "Never Again." From the time the thing which gave me the idea took place to the time I knew it was a story to the time I mailed it was from midnight to six the next afternoon.

I include these here because it might happen to you once or twice if you're lucky, and since it may be the best you ever do, I don't want you to miss it because you're scared. As I was. I called Bud Kelland and in a trembling voice told him all about it. "Maybe," I said, "it came so easy because it's no good. Do you think it's all right? Should I mail it?" There was a slight pause, then Bud said even more dryly than usual, "Mail it and thank God for it. That one came straight through without stopping is all."

Most of the time it will not be like that.

A short story is so many words of prose that deal with something happening to real people passed through the writer's imagination and viewpoint. Chekhov, probably most artistic critics' favorite short story writer, says, "Why write about a man getting into a submarine and going to the North Pole to reconcile himself to the world, while his beloved at that moment throws herself with a hysterical shriek from the belfry? All that is untrue and does not happen in real life. One must write about simple things: how Peter Semionovitch married Maria Ivanovna. That is all."

What is that "all," however?

From more than two hundred stories and over fifty years, believe me when I tell you that what "all" is and what it will be like are this.

8. Let us not belittle this. Or reduce it too quickly to the outward how to, which I propose to set down as best I can.

For now the writer begins to create.

In his head, heart, soul, blood stream, bowels, conscious and subconscious. The same way everything is created.

My son Richard, who has for some reason always understood about all this even before he was born, when he waited thirty days after the date set by the doctor for his arrival so I could finish a serial, once spoke some sage words, which I offer to any writer to pass on to the family. I heard him say outside my workroom door to someone who, though his business was important, was courteous enough not to want to interrupt me, "Oh, it's all right, we can go in, she's typing." This seemed to bewilder the caller, so Dick explained further. "When she's typing she knows it already, so you can't really interrupt her. It's when you can't hear a sound that you mustn't ever go in. Then she's thinking."

Of course no interruptions are best, but most of us have given up that dream—remember Edna Ferber's book which she dedicated to "My Mother, who thinks it doesn't interrupt if she whispers"—but on the whole Dick is right. As a rule, all you can lose after you start to write is a sentence, a phrase, the right word—and you can get them back. Before you start typing—or putting things down with a pen or pencil—you can lose the whole thing, and that is the time you should protect yourself from everyone except someone who really contributes a listening ear or a sounding board. Frequently then you are beyond interruption, you can hold long conversations and not remember a word, you can stare at people without seeing them, and in general behave like a writer hatching a story, and the publishing business is founded on the understanding that all writers are a little mad.

There is a period of time, with the rare exceptions already noted, between the idea and the time you start to write it down.

This is the period we are now going to deal with in how to write a short story and write it well enough to sell it.

Edna Ferber, unquestionably one of the all-time greats, says that the longer you have a story around the easier it is to write, like picking a peach that is ripe instead of tearing it off the tree green. This is usually true and is important to know, and to know also how to ripen a story to the best advantage.

To show you what elapsed time can be, how long and in what way it works, a few weeks ago I sold to *Good Housekeeping* a story which I called "Pig-in-a-Poke," though what it will be called when it is published I don't know, because our Mr. Mayes fancies his own titles, and I must say usually he's right. Like his questions, which reminds me that I should have explained that part of the gift is to ask the right author the right question—the ones he asks me are different, for instance, from the ones he asks John P. Marquand, or the hard-hitting and vivid Libbie Block or Faith Baldwin, or maybe even Daphne du Maurier.

I can give you an exact breakdown on "Pig-in-a-Poke," which you may have read or will read, I hope. You'll recognize it because it's about that.

Twenty-three years ago I gave a wedding for a young girl whose dead mother had been one of my dearest friends. The child spent the week before the wedding at my house and she seemed so shy and innocent that I felt her mother would wish me to do what I could to prepare her happily for her bridal night. As I began this, she gave me a sudden hostile look that made me realize I was too late, I wasn't about to tell her anything she didn't know and hadn't known for some time by experience.

Then as I stumbled on, trying to get myself off the hook, she began to cry.

So—that was the idea.

It never left me, and that is the point I want to make here. Once you get a flash like that, don't let it leave you. Install somewhere inside yourself a repository for ideas for short stories. Always write them down at once in a notebook, but that's just a small part of it—I use the notebook to jog my memory, to start the wheels going on something that appeals to me from it that perhaps I haven't thought of in a long time. For instance, just for fun a moment ago I peeked at mine and found these words: "New Moon Marriage." That's a Canadian story that Larry Trimble, the man who knew more about dogs than anybody, told me ten or fifteen years ago. I haven't thought about that one in quite a while but it suddenly latched on to something I heard yesterday and it's on the active file inside me again—it's a really good story, it seems to me now.

But put your ideas inside and this becomes the gestation period.

They grow.

More than that, if you train whatever it is inside you, these ideas magnetize to themselves whatever comes along that fits them. They reach out and pull in, sometimes without your own awareness, a word of dialogue, a certain gesture, some bit of business or minor character. "Rain," one of the most successful stories in all literary history, came to Somerset Maugham because of a girl who boarded his steamer in Honolulu after a raid on the red light district there. His note on her, he tells us in a brilliant preface to my favorite collection of his short stories and one I give for Christmas to all the young writers I know, *East and West*, was as follows: "Plump, pretty in a coarse fashion, perhaps not more than twenty-seven. She wore a white dress and a large white hat, long white boots from which the calves bulged in cotton stockings." Miss Thompson came alive in Maugham's short story long before we saw Jeanne Eagels in the role. A great deal had been added to Mr. Maugham's concept of her and the people around her before that.

My thoughts about the girl to whom I talked the night before her wedding were first annoyed, then sad. I thought, This is a moment every girl goes through. Life is so peculiar. It's only later that you understand what it means to have a wedding night, that you know what it should be like. Why is life the only thing in which you have to go back and start at the beginning every time and learn everything for yourself? A man who makes automobiles can take advantage of everything Henry Ford knew. But most everybody has to learn life by living it. Some examples—a few precepts—I fooled around with the story but it wouldn't work. It was a very green peach so I left it there.

Every now and again, by itself or on one of my trips through my notebook, it bobbed up. In those years I didn't see as much of younger people as I do now, I was interested in friends my own age, in their dramas, and incidentally in myself and what was happening to me, and quite a lot was, I was doing a great deal of newspaper work at that time. Our work naturally enough follows to some extent the stream of our life—or vice versa. When we write about Peter Semionovitch marrying Maria Ivanovna, we may be Peter and Maria, or they may be our best friends or later on we may be pure observers. But all the time the girl was in there, gathering moss and flesh and vitality. Once I wondered if it should be a girl and a maiden aunt, but that lacked guts.

About a year ago I heard a conversation. By this time life had become to me a spectator sport. I am an ardent fan. I wouldn't miss a game, I can root and weep and dance around goal posts still, but—more or less as a spectator. I began to enjoy listening to and watching young people because they were much more unpredictable than my own friends, new things were happening to them. I noted one thing. Girls at the universities whom I knew, friends of my sons and daughter and nephews and nieces, were contemplating pre-marital relations in an entirely different way than youngsters had in my day. I heard an intelligent young woman say gravely, "I think perhaps it's much wiser," and I thought, Oh, the poor things.

Then I thought, Ah, now is the time. That's the right approach to the story of the girl I gave the wedding to twenty-two years ago. It had taken history a while to catch up—but then of course there are thousands of variations on the theme. Such as the real life story of Evelyn Nesbit Thaw.

It took me about six days to find where to start the story, which always is and should be the most difficult part of writing it, and then about three days to finish it. Mathematically, I judge that the percentage of writing to elapsed time on this one would be fantastic, but certainly it paid off. Ideas always will. Just be patient and active inside with them. Naturally I expect to die with a full notebook, but aside from that, every idea I've had time to write has sold.

Of course this is not quite fair, for in the intervening years I have acquired more ease and speed and skill in using the tools of my trade, more than a newer writer can have, even granting a great natural aptitude, which sometimes the best story minds don't have and never acquire. I have never worked in a motion picture studio that didn't have three or four story men—idea men—under contract who contributed but couldn't put together some of the best stories. Who could always come up with an idea to save some other hard-working screen writer or dramatist.

What I want to say is that patience is a great asset to any short story writer. He ought to have enough ideas to keep some of them in the deep freeze for use later on.

Of a well-written and very amusing tale called " 'Twas the Night before Christmas," Paul Gallico says in his *Confessions*, "This one simply wouldn't jell and I tried everything until it began to haunt me. I worked on it, writing outline after outline, and none of them made sense. I could get it started, but I couldn't finish it. . . . I just had about given this story up—in fact, had forgotten about it—when suddenly one night during a symphony concert I was attending at Carnegie Hall the solution popped out of nowhere and the story simply rolled forth. I wrote out the ideas on the margin of the program and finished the piece within a week."

So, if after a month of trying, thinking, outlining, you can't or haven't been able to jell it, put it away and keep going to symphony concerts, I mean that. Nothing starts the creative flow in many writers like music.

However, Gallico had never forgotten the story, he'd just submerged it, left it to ripen, which it did. There is, believe me there is, there has to be, a force, a creative force beyond ourselves, we must give it a chance to operate.

There is something else about this incident that is important.

I was there when Jack Clements told that Christmas night story to Gallico. I've heard some wonderful storytellers: Wilson Mizner, Mark Kelly, James Cagney, Georgie Jessel; and Clements, a great newspaperman, was as good as any of them. He told that story in detail and had us wiping away the tears of mirth and honking like geese. But for a written story, they were all the wrong details. In my notebook are four or five stories I've heard the great Clements tell. The one about his mother and the time they served her son John beans for Sunday morning breakfast in the Marine Corps I know to be a classic. Then there was the time a girl Clements admired married another man and Clements, a reporter on the New York Journal, called the cops, the fire department, the morgue, Bellevue, the Society for Prevention of Cruelty to Animals, and any other agencies he could think of and gave them the address where she and her new husband were spending the night. I've never written one of these stories, nor have any of the other successful writers to whom Clements has told them except Gallico. They are too difficult to change, they are already complete in their own medium of the minstrel word. You are not trying to create a short story around a fragment, an idea, a theme, a character, an incident; you try to put down on paper the story as Clements told it, and the spoken word and the written word are altogether different. I never got a story from Mizner's brilliant conversation either, nor from Mark Kelly's. They are all too good. You will get more from the guy who stumbles along and leaves behind merely something for you to work from.

Never try to get too close to the truth. Never allow yourself to tell a story exactly as it happened. It won't come off if you do. A painter makes a portrait a third larger than life to make it come out life-size. When he makes a sketch, he puts in everything. From that he eliminates, rearranges, highlights, adds or subtracts what he needs. There must always be room as you move from facts to fiction for the creative glory to do its work.

Could be Clements had already done all the creative work.

A writer has to make a short story complete in itself.

The action must all be there, whether it is told in a sentence of flashback or is part of the narrative. So that when the idea presents itself it is necessary to find out whether the idea will and can be told in the length in which a short story is publishable. The first full-length serial I did was from a short story Ray Long rejected. A week later he wired me, "I know what is wrong with 'The Skyrocket.' You can't tell it in a short story. Start on it as a serial."

So there are the stories that you put away and add to inside, for weeks or years. There are the ones on which you work at once and pretty definitely to arrange the plot.

I do not think plot is my strong point. But Jack O'Connell says that is because I do not know what a plot is and that I have it confused with detective stories. This could be. Jack says that a yarn of mine called "The Crime of Daphne Rutledge," which appeared in *Cosmopolitan*, is as good an example of short story plot as can be shown and complimented me—as Mr. Maugham says somewhere, we authors are simply childish creatures and we treasure a word of praise from those who buy our wares—by saying that he did not know a young writer who could do it, that most of them stuck to moods because they were afraid to plot, and that was one reason so many of the stories sent in to editors today were lousy—my word, not his.

As far as I know, a plot is simply how you tell the story.

After you select your character or your theme or your incident or whatever the idea was in the beginning, you must invent a tale.

This is the plot.

Maybe we ought to start a new chapter for plots. They are very important of course, and I get so interested in them that once in a while I forget to end a chapter and begin a new one. Short stories are my hobby as well as my profession, as you may have guessed.

9. The thing the reader gets from a short story must, in part, be what the writer sees, his own way of looking at people, his own reactions to the world. The picture he sets down in character, action, and plot is his view of life as it has passed through his mind, his imagination, and it must bear his imprint. Not style—that is a product of himself in most instances—but his philosophy, his own character, his opinion about many things. While each of his characters expresses his or her own feelings and thoughts, there is always an over-all patina of the writer.

The value a writer's inner thoughts and emotions give to a story are a plus. But he must have them or he will never be topflight.

Nor is this a matter of youth or age. I read a short story the other day by Françoise Sagan, the author of *Bonjour Tristesse*, in one of the expensive fashion magazines, I don't remember which one. The story exhibits the same desperate young ignorance and lack of scope that the novel shows, but it expresses it, it expresses an aching pain and loneliness that distrusts life and makes the reader remember just how desperate and lonely youth, which as yet has no understanding at all of time or the future or compensations or change, can be. The character, the viewpoint, of this teen-age French girl vibrates like echoes of "Melancholy Baby" from every paragraph.

She has not been afraid to write as she sees.

That is the secret of her success.

A reader picks his writers as he does his friends, because he likes and is interested in them, in what they say, stand for, convey, as well as for the entertainment of the story itself. The writer does come through. Therefore it is well for the writer to learn to be himself, to be honest in his viewpoint of his story and characters.

But whatever is behind it of the writer's personality and thought, a story must be *told*.

I have a fondness myself for stories that have a beginning, a middle, and an end, and in which something happens. What are known as mood stories leave me cold, with a definite impression that I have been insulted by a writer who either wouldn't take the trouble or hadn't the ability to work out his plot, his way of telling his story, but wished me, the reader, to do his work for him. We have learned to settle for a good deal of this anemic bilge, though I have not spoken with anyone who likes it on the whole. The greatest disservice done the short story in America in years, in this century, has been by *The New Yorker*, and it wasn't *The New Yorker's* fault. They were all right. It was their imitators who caused the damage. A magazine with definite space limitations, which is designed, and always has been, for a very special and relatively small audience, that New York audience which is different, *The New Yorker* established its aura and its content and has maintained them at a high level. Some of the short stories it has published, if you like that school, are little gems. No doubt of that. Unfortunately, the lazy young writers who wouldn't bother to work out a plausible story with which to express an idea hooked on to this pattern and began to flood the market with half-baked mood, one-incident-in-his-life, stream-of-consciousness, character-sketch stories of which all too many reminded me of a bad-mannered monkey I used to know up at the Hearst ranch. *The New Yorker* type piece well done by Sally Benson, or Dorothy Parker, or Kay Boyle or Nancy Hale or Ruth McKenney, Arthur Kober, or Clarence Day is one thing, but the other is as phony and dishonest as bad blank verse written because the poet is too lazy to make it rhyme.

We are going to have to get down to business and leave this to those who really express themselves best in this Chekhov school if the short story is to be again in America what it should be, derived perhaps more from Mark Twain and Hawthorne.

I am going to quote here from a letter written me the other day—at my request—by John Reese.

This is a break for my readers. For John is my pick of the newer writers. Briefly, when he was a kid he hit a gold mine in the pulps, and was averaging around a hundred to a hundred and fifty dollars a week for a year or two. That vein ran out, of course, but he'd learned a lot, and after batting around the country as a labor leader, taxi driver, and newspaperman, he got married and, to add to his income, began to write for the pulps again. In the past two or three years he has had thirty-seven short stories and two novelettes in *The Saturday Evening Post*, and he is a very good example of a man who can invent an interesting, plausible story to go with his ideas.

Because he is of the new school, the younger school, I think his ideas are extraordinarily valuable.

Some of his stories are run-of-the-mill, but they always give entertainment value received. He's a professional writer and has one of those wives, Maggie, and three of my favorite children. Some of John's stories are as fine as they come. In my opinion, the great short stories are written by honest professional writers, though they may hit that peak only two or three times in an entire career. I have always regarded John as an expert on plot and story invention, so I was a little surprised at what he has to say here. I mean his method is exactly the same as mine.

John Reese says:

> *I have always contended that all stories start with a character and you plot from there. I used to have a trick I used in pressrooms. I would get roped into the old discussion of how to write, and sooner or later some reporter would say the ancient line, "I could write, I know, except I can't plot." My answer was always, "Writing is plotting. If you can't plot, you can't write. Any jerk can learn to manipulate a vocabulary enough*

to express a given thought, but in too many cases he hasn't got a thought. To come up with the thoughts around an idea, that is plotting. And the gimmick in the short story plot is not the plot, it's only an outgrowth of characterization, and it is not valid if it tries to be anything else."

Then I would always offer to prove how you start with a character. I would say, "Give me a character, any kind of a real, basic, human character, and we'll sit right down now and plot a story. The difference between us is that I'll work, I'll write it and sell it and show you a check." Several times I have made that bluff and never have I fallen down—and never have they done anything about it. Work.

That's why I always resent those people who give you what they call a great idea for a story which consists of a situation, nothing more. For instance: A perfectly respectable man is found dead on his front lawn by his next-door neighbor in an exclusive residential district with a brief case clutched in his hand and in it packaged twenty thousand dollars in small bills that can be definitely traced to a big, unsolved extortion case. I had this idea given to me in just this form some time back.

It's a good, sound situation with the shock value I like in an opening. But that's all it is and I am immediately confronted by what I insist is the basic problem of plotting—that of characterization. The whole situation changes as a slight change occurs in your concept of any of the characters. A good man will react differently to a given situation than a bad man. A brave man's reflexes are different than a coward's. A man who is happily married will behave differently in a given set of circumstances than a man who thinks his wife is *carrying on an affair with his best friend. So if your story starts with a situation, you go at once to the characters and see what about them, so it really starts with characters before you move.*

What a writer has to say is his particular feel about the characters involved. You and I, both making our living at this business, can hear Jim Richardson come up with an idea with entirely different reactions. It invokes different memories. To me, it may mean only a cute gimmick that has no warmth to it. You, who have perhaps known some person who fitted that or bore some resemblance to this lay figure, make take off on it.

I remember one idea we both heard which left me cold, an artificial, stagy situation used a million times about somebody trying to force his dying wishes on a future generation. I thought of it in masculine terms. You thought of it as a woman's story and came up with a warm, tender story of a dying woman's love for her daughter. You were able, in short, to make it a story of characters.

Plotting to me is a myth and it's a shame to teach anyone otherwise. Take the story of The Prodigal Son, the best and most famous of the "short shorts" in classical literature. The theorists would surely go crazy trying to break this story down in terms of suspense, story arch, bridge, climax, and whatever those things are. This is a successful short story, as all Jesus' were, because it is fundamentally a brilliant exploit in characterization. What can happen when the wastrel son returns home? This situation is ripe with dramatic possibilities. The story is a success because of the character of the father, whose simple, direct solution has not only the element of surprise for the reader but the emo-

tional kick of a truly happy ending—all the happier, by the way, because of the element of surprise. The reader expects the son to get the business, or at least be put to some kind of a test to see what his future behavior is likely to be. The father wants the kid to get a break, but nobody could blame him for saying, "Look, Son, you've made an awful mess of your life and caused me a lot of misery. I wonder if you've got the stuff it takes to be a man. Here's what I'm going to do . . ." And at this point your average plotter would start building up an intricate and artificial plot in which the young prodigal is put to some kind of a test, probably without knowing it. Had this been done in the original version, the story would have been forgotten nineteen hundred years ago. But because it is a great story of fundamental characterization, basic and simple and sound, it has survived.

Which brings me to a point I have long labored—a successful writer needs two things only: 1. Knowledge of and respect for the English language. 2. Detailed, rich, intimate knowledge of human nature, and he had better set about getting that rather than learning how to write. Without both these things, whatever else it may have, a writer's work is trite and valueless.

As for writing for the Post, its editors tell me that they don't know what the public wants, they only know what it will take. I don't know what the editors want, but I have a vague idea what they'll take. First, they want tight writing, more story than has ever been crammed into a given number of words before. The stories you see in the Post every week would have required fifteen thousand words to write fifty years ago. Our language has undergone a sensitive, racy refinement *in those past fifty years, and it is necessary to abide by it.*

You asked me what I think is the best short story ever written. I would say—have to say—it's one of O. Henry's little-known and most neglected ones, "The Indian Summer of Dry Valley Johnson." It's also the best love story in the English language.

The best advice I could give a beginning writer, I think, is be yourself. Write the story that you want to write. It's true at first it may not fit any known magazine and will be wasted. But sooner or later, by writing what you want to write, you'll get those dismal, low-key, offbeat stories every youth has in him out of your system and you'll start writing about more writable people. And the wasted effort, the stories thrown into the wastebasket, the time lost, won't add up to nearly as costly an amount as trying to write to any formula. It's a long tough row to hoe, but you'll get there quicker and with less confusion and loss by writing the stories that have an emotional kick to them.

I guess the best advice I could give would be what I once heard you tell a class. Take three years off, get a job that allows you to eat, and do nothing but read. It is truly astounding with the alleged growth in education how little the average man or woman who wants to write has read.

You can't stop a man who really wants to write. He has something to say, something he has to say or bust. So those of us who know what a tough road this is must give him a hand. What information we have. There are no short cuts, no magic formulas, no tricks. But those of us who have been on the road may help make a map or two, I suppose.

So John Reese begins as I do, with character. That is to say, even if the initial springboard should be a theme or a situation, no actual work can be done in your mind on the story until the characters are selected, for the plotting must be controlled by who and what the characters are. Unless this is plain, you will have a false and artificial story.

John speaks of my advice to a class about reading.

I would like to give you a list of required reading for which you should find time.

My same little chambermaid here at my hide-out inn, the one who objected to so many pieces of yellow paper on the floor every morning—every morning—also said to me one day, "Do you have to have all these books? Why do you leave them on the floor too? You have bring with you a bookcase, no?"

I said that I did have to have all these books, the same way she had to have a vacuum cleaner and a sort of tin basket to carry rags and cleanser and brushes in, the books were my tools, part of my work. And I said in spite of bringing a bookcase, a portable one which I can carry everywhere, I left them on the floor because then I could leave them open at the place where I wanted them to be. This did not seem to make much sense to her and maybe it doesn't to you. But it ought to.

Among the books which I have to have, I find—looking them over:

> All the Kipling short stories
> *The Complete Short Stories* of Maupassant
> *East and West,* by Somerset Maugham

The Summing Up by Somerset Maugham
The Complete Sherlock Holmes, by Conan Doyle
Collected Stories of Katherine Mansfield
Guys and Dolls, by Damon Runyon
The Round Up, by Ring Lardner
Modern English Readings, edited by Roger Sherman Loomis and Donald Lemen Clark
Reading I've Liked, by Clifton Fadiman
The Woollcott Reader
Woollcott's Second Reader
Liffey Lane, by Maura Laverty
A Treasury of Great Poems, by Louis Untermeyer
The First and Second Glencannon Omnibuses, by Guy Gilpatric
The Golden Argosy, edited by Van H. Cartmell and Charles Grayson (the best of the anthologies)
Confessions of a Story Writer, by Paul Gallico
Letters from a Self-Made Merchant to His Son, by George Horace Lorimer
All of O. Henry's works
Modern Parables, by Fulton Oursler
The Modern Library *Great Modern Short Stories,* edited by Bennett Cerf
The short stories of Chekhov
Meet Mr. Fortune, by H. C. Bailey
Introduction to Modern English and American Literature, by Somerset Maugham
Farewell to Sport, by Paul Gallico
At Sallygap and Other Stories, by Mary Lavin
Penrod, by Booth Tarkington
Letters of Edna St. Vincent Millay
The short stories of Dorothy Parker
A Lost Lady, by Willa Cather

A Pedlar's Pack, by Elizabeth Goudge
Golden Skylark " " "
North to the Orient, by Anne Morrow Lindbergh
Listen, the Wind " " " "
Gift from the Sea " " " "
Van Loon's Lives, by Hendrik Willem Van Loon
Essays of Ralph Waldo Emerson
Ethan Frome, by Edith Wharton
The Man That Corrupted Hadleyburg, by Mark Twain
The Little World of Don Camillo, by Giovanni Guareschi
To Be a Pilgrim, by Joyce Cary
Black Lamb and Grey Falcon, by Rebecca West
The Meaning of Treason " " "
The Maltese Falcon, by Dashiell Hammett
The Saturday Evening Post Treasury
The New Yorker Book of War Pieces
The Spectator, by Addison and Steele
Robinson Crusoe, by Daniel Defoe
Flight to Arras, by Antoine de St. Exupéry
Indigo Bunting, by Vincent Sheean
Eminent Victorians, by Lytton Strachey
Goodbye, Mr. Chips, by James Hilton
Six Novels of the Supernatural, edited by Edward Wagen-
    knecht
Star Reporters, and 34 of Their Stories, by Ward Greene
Certain People of Importance by Kathleen Norris
Little Ships " " "
Grimm's Fairy Tales
Aesop's Fables
The Wizard of Oz, by L. Frank Baum
archy and mehitabel, by Don Marquis
Wolfville, by Alfred Henry Lewis

Uncle Remus, His Songs and His Sayings, by Joel
  Chandler Harris
Alice in Wonderland, by Lewis Carroll
The Arabian Nights
Nothing but Wodehouse, edited by Ogden Nash
A Walk in the Sun, by Harry Brown
The Country of the Pointed Firs, by Sarah Jewett
Short novels of Henry James
Pilgrim's Progress, by John Bunyan
Adventurers All (the Richard Hannay omnibus), by John
  Buchan
All of Jane Austen's works
Three Kingdoms, by Storm Jameson
Romeo and Juliet, Hamlet, A Midsummer Night's Dream,
  and *Macbeth*
Pickwick Papers
The Bible

All of these are available in libraries, and in the various col-
lections are such musts in short stories as "The Happy Hypo-
crite," by Max Beerbohm, "Roman Fever," by Edith Wharton,
"The Story of the Other Wise Man," by Henry Van Dyke,
"The Gift," by John Steinbeck, "The Chink and the Child,"
by Thomas Burke, "Old Man Minnick," by Edna Ferber, "The
Lady or the Tiger?" by Frank Stockton, "Monsieur Beaucaire,"
by Booth Tarkington, Sherwood Anderson's "I'm a Fool."

I would like to try to explain what these mean to me and
why I require them as reading by any sincere would-be writer
and why I do not travel anywhere without at least some of
them—and usually all of them.

To ignore them would be as though an architect said, "I will never look at a house or building that has ever been put up." Or as though a musician refused to go to a concert to hear Mozart and Beethoven. Or an electrician refused to recognize or utilize the works of Edison.

Here it is possible to find the structure and method of every kind of a short story that ever has been or ever will be conceived. These writers over the years, many of them as inspired as anybody can be, have ironed out some of the stresses and strains, they have discarded the impossibles, they have established certain patterns just as Mozart established them in the world of music. They hold high the torches of their spirit and their work. Why should we refuse to see by that light?

Once in a story conference at Metro-Goldwyn-Mayer when I was a member of the story board I kept trying to explain to a script writer why I didn't like what he had done. It is always very delicate and difficult to criticize a fellow craftsman's work and I know all too well how maddening it is when an editor says, "I just don't like it," and gives you nothing constructive to go on. Of course there is always the possibility that he just doesn't like it or it just isn't good enough, but you always hope for something to indicate that you can repair or redo it.

Finally I said, "Look—you can't write for Clark Gable in waltz time."

Bless him, the script writer accepted this with gratitude and good will and went off to put it in march tempo or symphonic style. He knew what I meant immediately.

It is not stealing anything to write music in march time. If you are going to do just that, you do not sit around putting waltz records on the phonograph. If you do, you will get your ear full of waltz time and then you are in trouble. No, no. You put on Sousa marches. Not that the composer means to, or will or can, steal a note, a bar, a melody, or chord. But he gets his soul and mind and ear full of the right time, the right tempo.

When you start the idea of a short story, there is always a tempo to it. A feel. You have to read. Every writer reads as he breathes or eats—from necessity. Like Somerset Maugham, he carries a book bag. Or locates the public library. When the short story starts and the tempo is apparent, I decide who would have written this short story best. Mrs. Wharton? Steinbeck? Ben Hecht? Sally Benson? Maugham? Runyon? Henry James? The world is wide. Once I get it figured out, I try to get that style and tempo into my ear. My insides. Try to get it to permeate that from which the story comes when I begin to write it.

Also it is essential to enrich your storehouse, to keep it well stocked. The English language is truly a great and flexible instrument. Reading the works of all these writers fills you with a sense of its power. Phrases stick. One of the first exercises I set my classes—and often young writers who come to me—is to write down swiftly and without pause fifty good quotations. I don't care whether they are from the Bible or *Alice* or Joe Palooka or Keats or Ogden Nash. They are part of the enrichment of your everyday use of the language. I have always felt that the creative writing courses and the schools of creative writing could spend more time on reading and vocabulary if they could get the students to sit still for it. A little practice and warm-up in these fields pays off big. I'd like to offer this above list of required reading to students and say that I have learned from it maybe some 35 per cent of what has made me a successful short story writer. Also I once taught a class at Stephens College and we worked for three whole days on vocabulary. It was no use starting to write. These college freshmen didn't have enough words to do a respectable fourth-grade composition. There are *words*, you know. The wrong ones, the ones that will do, and the right ones. In three days we got 287 synonyms for the catchword of the moment, which was "swell." On the other hand, if your character is a girl who says "swell" for exciting, magnificent, romantic, beautiful, kind, successful, gay, she will have to say "swell" ninety-nine times in one short story.

But there are those writers of whom you hear that they spend days on a paragraph or often seeking the right words.

I myself wear out at least one Thesaurus a year and feel that I owe as much to M. Roget as to anyone who ever lived. Sometimes a word is so vital that you can spend hours pursuing it, looking for a fresh one—or a more completely accurate one—words are so wonderful, they have such beauty. Vocabulary—the use of words, familiarity with hundreds and thousands of them—can be learned. From books. By listening. I don't mean big words, abstruse words, difficult words. No, no. Just the right words.

Alexander Woollcott's *While Rome Burns* will repay a lot of vocabulary study. He has a unique choice of words. "Nor did he relish a blind plunge into the thorny shrubbery beneath his window and a barefoot scamper across the frosty turf." As you see, 'tis the word "scamper," particularly in a ghost story, that does it. "A hoarse bell which, from the clock tower, had been contemptuously scattering the hours like coins ever since Henry VIII was a rosy stripling." Also in *When Rome Burns* he said, in speaking of his adored Dorothy Parker, "You see, she is so odd a blend of Little Nell and Lady Macbeth. It is not so much the familiar phenomenon of a hand of steel in a velvet glove as a lacy sleeve with a bottle of vitriol concealed in its folds. She has the gentlest, most disarming demeanor of anyone I know. Don't you remember sweet Alice, Ben Bolt? Sweet Alice wept with delight, as I recall, when you gave her a smile and, if memory serves, trembled with fear at your frown. Well, compared to Dorothy Parker, sweet Alice was a roughshod bully trampling down all opposition."

Do you see what I mean by knowledge of quotations? Of background? Not to quote, but to weave into the warp and woof of your language, to embellish and spangle and clarify the cloth of your language. Little Nell and Lady Macbeth, the steel hand in the velvet glove, sweet Alice, Ben Bolt. These should be as much a part of your written word as the "a" and "if," "by" or "but."

I regard Rebecca West's *Black Lamb and Grey Falcon* as the finest use of English in our century. As well as one of the great books.

There are of course trade and local vocabularies, such as Runyon's Broadwayese or Harry Brown's army talk in *A Walk in the Sun*. Writing of people and places you know should be, if you listen, train your ear to listen, part of an ability to characterize quickly. If your idea has a locality, or flashbacks to a locality, foreign to you, it is perfectly legitimate to research for it in other people's books or on the scene. I once spent weeks around the old Newark airport making friends with commercial airlines pilots to do half a dozen stories for Fulton Oursler. One way to make old plots new is to lay them in a new, exciting locality or industrial or professional setting. Maupassant, O. Henry, and Sherwood Anderson used many of the same situations, but they looked very, very different laid in Paris, New York, and Winesburg, Ohio, and told about the people who lived in these places.

The tight writing which John Reese speaks of must be taken very seriously today. From fifteen thousand to five thousand words to tell a short story is a major change. Of course, the new writer accepts five thousand, never having known any different, but the need for tight writing is there just the same.

My last murder trial for INS and the Los Angeles *Examiner*, the Overell case in Santa Ana, California, I found myself committed after I arrived to *six hundred* words for my daily feature. To one accustomed to two thousand minimum, this was a

bitter blow. I will tell you what I did because I suggest you
follow it. This new tight style is best executed by the really
competent columnists. Winchell had a lot to do with inaugu-
ration and popularity. A master of this style second to none is
Herb Stein, Hollywood columnist for *Racing Form*, the New
York *Morning Telegraph*, among others. I not only read many
of Herb's columns but, since he is a friend of mine, asked him
to help me. It was miraculous. I managed to say all I had to
say in six hundred words, though of course it took me much
longer to write. The shorter the longer, in all writing. I recommend Mr. Stein's column to your careful attention. This may
not be reading Swift or Dryden, as Mr. Maugham says he did,
but at the present market it will be considerably more valuable.
You will see there, too, what vocabulary means. In such short
space the words must tell. No wastage. The right short word.
The right simple word. Remember the necessity of the high
price of paper and the rise in labor costs were the mother of
this new literary school. Tell it short, there just isn't room.
Do things like Herb's "This is D-Departure Day for M-G-M
studio ad-exploitation topper Frank Whitbeck, pension-
pasturing after better than quarter century in show biz that
spans from gas to neon. He leaves Metro with a grand canyon
it probably will never fill. After Whitbeck accordions some
possessions he'll Remington his Memoirs."

The short story is more sculpture than painting. Always
chip-chip-chipping away. I will tell you one of my few trade
secrets. Of course it is always better to write long and then cut

and tighten, it gives you a richer product, but you must learn to cut. It hurts, too. I always cut when I am as tired as it is possible for me to get. When my eyes burn and my back aches and my typewriter chair is the rack, I find that anything I just plain can't bear to cut so it will shorten the time before I can go to bed ought to stay in. You don't need to worry about cutting too close. That never happens. Something won't let you, that's the point. But by the time you finish this last cut under those circumstances, all your fancy writing and your unnecessary (favorite) words are where the chambermaid will complain about 'em in the morning! Which in short story writing is where they belong.

If you keep my list of books around you, I guarantee that there is no story you can think up for which there isn't a style in these volumes.

All this means what I have always said:

Anybody can learn to write.

If he will read, work, keep at it, study, write and write and write and cut and cut and cut.

Ruthlessly.

Last summer I worked with a brilliant woman who had a magnificent story to tell and just had to tell it. I thought it was a story of such importance that I wanted to give a hand— a story of a woman's true conversion to Christianity, undoubtedly the most vital subject of our time. She had just junked a complete version when we started, and I'll say this for her, she had the guts and stamina of the true Christian bent on serving the Lord. But after three long, hot months—typing was new to her and it took her hours instead of minutes—she brought me the last page—everything had been okayed up to then.

It was dreadful.

I said so, and there was a silence and I looked up. She was weeping bucketfuls, and I could see that the only reason she didn't use the very extensive vocabulary she'd possessed before she was saved on me was because she couldn't speak. She was really pooped.

Now I am as fond of this gal as I can be and I try to be a Christian myself. But I remember I didn't care in the slightest. I said to myself, *What's the matter with her? She has a great story and she now has to go and rewrite the last page, maybe once, maybe ten times, maybe fifty. Let's get on with it, can't let down now.* I had no compassion at all. The only thing I can say for myself is that it would not have entered my head to do anything different to myself. I was actually paying her a high compliment. It takes that kind of guts in the pinches, that kind of self-discipline, and if you aren't prepared for it, find a pleasant job with a concern that has good retirement pay—this isn't for you.

The story, incidentally, has scared the wits out of publishers so far. Someday it will find one with sufficient courage and faith in the Master, and then you'll read something. It has never occurred to me to doubt it because that would be to see some of the best writing unpublished, and it never happens.

10.

There is one more side to writing important enough to have a chapter to itself, because I find it's the one consistent thing I know about writing and construction.

I have always believed that what you say is more important than how you say it. Certainly it is better to write well than to write badly, but too often I find people worrying desperately about how to say something that isn't worth saying anyhow. I have wished more time was spent on thinking, feeling, knowing people, and less on the thought of style and construction, which has to be second at least. No amount of technique can repair an engine that isn't under the hood, and no glory of style, knack with words, or fancy writing can conceal the horrid barrenness and vacuum where sincerity, passion, and a great need and desire to tell a story that will make people laugh or cry or fight ought to be.

Often that desire will develop its own strokes, as Helen Wills explained a game of tennis would do for her. I like hot writing, myself, which is, I suppose, the newspaper training.

But a professional writer must write often

when the urge isn't hot. He will sometimes have the urge and the desire and yet they will run head on into lethargy, inertia, opposition, rebellion, and despair. This must be faced by anyone who thinks of selling enough short stories to make a living, of becoming a pro.

The most helpful words I have ever heard on this subject were said to me many years ago by Charlie Chaplin and must carry weight because of his own supreme artistry, whatever his politics may now have become.

"You start," he said, "with spontaneity, pure spontaneity. It bubbles, it's glorious, and of course it captures people. You haven't the faintest idea how you do it. That lasts a little while. Then you begin to develop technique. You have to, for there are times when the spontaneity betrays and deserts you. You develop the technique—and the first thing you know it's all you have, the spontaneity is gone, it seems, for good. Then you must learn to combine the two. Those who can do this with both at their peak are geniuses. And on down the scale in the quality they produce. But if you intend to make a life's work of your art, your talent, you must, through great self-discipline and control and balance, learn to combine spontaneity and technique."

Spontaneity is the gift of God and must be prayed for.

Technique can be learned.

The most crucial technical approach to a short story is where you start it.

This I know.

You have so little room, anyhow. You must write so tight and tell so much. Everything in the way your story unfolds depends on finding exactly the point at which to begin it. Naturally, the shorter you can keep the space in which the action takes place, the less time elapses, the better. Take Hemingway's great story, "The Killers." "The door of Henry's lunchroom opened and two men came in. They sat down at the counter." A few hours later George says, "Well, you better not think about it." Anything we need to know is told in sentences of flashback. "We're killing him for a friend. Just to oblige a friend, bright boy." There is also Mr. Hemingway's "The Short Happy Life of Francis Macomber." "It was now lunch time and they were all sitting under the double green fly of the dining tent, pretending that nothing had happened."

Or Willa Cather's "Paul's Case," a terrible story which everybody who deals with youth should be made to read by law. "It was Paul's afternoon to appear before the faculty of the Pittsburgh High School to account for his various misdemeanors." Some time passes then before the dreadful end, but that is the only place to start it.

Then there is Mary Lavin's "Love Is for Lovers." "At the noncommittal age of forty-four, Mathew Simmins began to think about marriage." Or Bret Harte's famous "The Outcasts of Poker Flat." "As Mr. John Oakhurst, gambler, stepped into the main street of Poker Flat on the morning of the twenty-third of November, 1850, he was conscious of a change in its moral atmosphere since the preceding night." Or Steinbeck's "The Gift." "At daybreak, Billy Buck emerged from the bunk-house and stood for a moment on the porch looking up at the sky." And Dorothy Parker's "Big Blonde," which begins, "Hazel Morse was a large, fair woman of the type that incites men when they use the word 'blonde' to click their tongues and wag their heads roguishly."

Not only are these all intriguing, irresistible opening lines, hooks, but you are now right in the story. Right with the character. Here and now.

Kipling uses another method in "The Incarnation of Krishna Mulvaney" which can be very useful. "Once upon a time, very far from England, there lived three men who loved each other so greatly that neither man nor woman could come between them. They were in no sense refined, nor to be admitted to the outer-door mats of decent folk, because they happened to be private soldiers in Her Majesty's Army." There are then two pages which introduce Mulvaney and Learoyd and Ortheris—Soldiers Three—and then we come to "Omitting all else, this tale begins with the Lamentable Thirst that was at the beginning of First Causes. Never was such a thirst—Mulvaney told me so."

Maupassant uses much the same unfoldment in "Ball of Fat." "For many days now the fag end of the army had been straggling through the town." And three pages later, "Then, a large diligence with four horses having been engaged for this

journey and ten persons having engaged seats in it, it was re-
solved to set out on Tuesday morning before daylight in order
to escape observation."

This is also Maugham's usual style—a wide scope in setting
the general scene and then narrowing the focus to the character
or characters of the story itself. But Maugham admits that he
was greatly influenced by a long youthful study of Maupassant.

If you will study these stories, you will see that each one
begins at the precise moment that gives it the best leverage, as
it were. Naturally, no one even contemplates beginning a short
story until the end is clear as crystal. The one sure way to
crack up anything is not to know where you're going to land.
I often write the last paragraph and pin it on the curtain, where
I can see it. This is simple, for it has to happen in your head
to make a plausible, believable story—that is part of the plotting. Nearly always, with me, part of the spontaneity.

But where to begin?

This is the superlative of technique. It is the whole matter
of timing—of time and space and distance. For between that
first line and the ending you must tell your story. There must
be no tag ends. There must be no unanswered questions about
anything that happens or any of the people it happens to. You
will have no room for long, wordy explanations. No space to
repair errors. The furniture has to fit in *this* room.

I do not think that more than six times in two hundred
stories and fifty years I have known what was going to happen
between those two points—not all of it anyhow. You draw on

the reservoir of your memory and your experience and your urge and desire, and often unexpected things come forth. Nobody knows better than most writers that you don't do it all. Ever. But you must tune in to the right station, you must dial the right number or what comes forth at the call won't fit. The response won't be clear and definite. I remember very well my own utter amazement at a line in a short story of mine called "His Birthday." It made the story. There was a character in it I hadn't liked much and yet I felt the reader ought to. A loudmouthed noisy guy who was getting up a contest for the best house decoration in the development for Christmas. He seemed to me as I got to know him better one of those objectionable people who represent all that has made us forget that Christmas is His birthday. But in the first draft of the story were these lines of dialogue, which my brash guy spoke to the young couple who were the main characters: "Well, we'd better run along. Hope you'll forgive me making such a fuss and all about this contest but you know how Christmas is at our house. Our boy—he'd of been eleven this Christmas." Don't ask me where that came from. It was never in any plan or thought I had for the story.

Lovely things can come to pass. Lines of dialogue you hear. Bits of business you stored away years ago and that have ripened. A laugh you needed. Smooth progression and clear, clean scenes.

If you start at the right place.

If you don't, the whole story gets out of gear and stays that way. You keep trying to get it in the groove and it won't go.

Each story is different, so no one can tell anyone else just how to do it. In a sense, it's a matter of measurement. How far back from the ending do you go? Where does the actual story you are going to tell begin? Not the character formation and development, not the background, but the actual space in time which your action occupies. A few hours? A week? A month? If it's hours, you're lucky. Days okay. More than that, it gets tougher and tougher to handle. But, as in "The Snows of Kilimanjaro," once you have set that and have your right moment of starting it, then you can skitter back a thousand years if you want to.

Pace, I suppose, is another word for it.

I have another Christmas story—Christmas is a specially favorite time for me. My father loved Christmas. It has been a blessed time for all our family. I've done two Christmas stories that have been much loved. "Unto Us" and "His Birthday." I have another now that's better than either one of them. The trouble is I don't know yet where to start it.

Eddie Arcaro told me once that Willie Shoemaker is the greatest jockey who ever lived because, Eddie said, "Willie is such a patient boy." That seemed to me an odd quality to give greatness to a jockey who rides races in minutes, seconds, but Eddie said, "Nobody can ever push Willie into making a move before he and his horse are ready."

Patience is just as essential to a good short story writer. You have to learn to wait and not let anybody push you into making a move until you and your story are ready. I fouled up on that twice last year. So I had to put them away anyhow.

Patience is something I was born without.

But I've learned.

If you want to know how to write a short story you'd better begin now.

11.

Plotting is working out what happens to your characters as you unfold the story you have to tell about them.

Plotting, we have discovered, is mostly character.

To plot is to determine how characters would react to situations and each other. Or, since we need certain reactions from them, to determine or invent or dream up the occurrences or business or sights or sounds which would produce the anger or tenderness or humor or niggardliness or jealousy that is necessary to unfold your story. I once, for instance, used a man's jealousy of himself to prove a point in his opinion of his wife. Because I wanted all the sympathy to be with the wife, I couldn't introduce another man and get quite the same effect. But if the idea that his wife could dance, sing, and lose all sense of propriety with him on the beach convinced the husband that she had a wanton character—and he was that kind of a man—then he could tell her by his actions that he didn't think she was a nice woman.

Look at the consistency of the character of the father in the story of the prodigal son. *Give me the portion of goods that falleth to* me, the son said. The father gave it to him. Without argument, protest, haggling, or advice. Obviously the father was wise enough to know that sons do not on the whole listen to the advice of their fathers at the moment when they are asking for the portion of their goods. Also he must have known that every man has to learn about life for and by himself, especially concerning money. So with loving generosity he handed over the portion and the son went off and ended up with the husks and the swine, which are pretty easy to find nowadays, as they were then. But the teller of this tale had a great value in the character of the father at the moment he handed over that portion. For it was the memory of that loving kindness, that generosity, that father he had known for years in his house and with his servants that at last turned the prodigal son home. Lots of prodigals don't ever go home, you know. They remember the advice the fathers gave. They remember the look of distrust, they know that when they get home their welcome will be I told you so. And I warned you. If you'd done as I said in the first place—and now look at you. Oh yes. Let the poor guy in, maybe. But, as Drummond says in "The Greatest Thing in the World," many people are kept out of heaven by the unlovely character of those who claim to be already there. So that the power of the plotting of the story of the prodigal son lies in the character of the father.

Three things go into plotting the character.

Let's call them present observation, memory, and invention or intuition.

By present observation I mean reporting.

If I decide to do the story about the truck driver and the pretty girl and the fluttering mother I saw from my window the other day, I may have to talk with some truck driver, though I don't think I would. I do a great deal of driving and I see a large number of truck drivers, of whom as a rule I am very fond because they drive so much better than amateurs and you know they are not going to turn left in front of you after signaling right. As I look at their faces I find they are as different from each other as the same number of men who are bankers or college presidents or automobile salesmen. I find to my surprise that there are no "typical" truck drivers, they are men driving trucks just as doctors are men practicing medicine, so any character can be found among them. However, I would undoubtedly need some trade dialogue, hours, distances, future plans, and ambitions—all that is reporting, or present observation, and is part of how your character lives, and therefore part of plotting.

Very often observation or reporting is necessary for clothes, which is why I have magazines such as *Harper's Bazaar, Vogue* and *Town and Country*. My own clothes long ago reached a standard pattern based on what is the least trouble, but I still love to look at the new styles and I must know all the quirks and quiddles of modern fashions. Not only to dress my characters as they would be dressed, but for their own thinking and reactions, since clothes are a deep part of many women's character. I have one on my mind right now, for instance—

but that is another story, I hope. Also music. As music is so often part of life, it must be part of stories. I always listen, and report, the Hit Parade. Have ever since Frank Sinatra was the singer on it. In my present, quiet, hard-working life this is my best method of keeping in touch with popular music, what my characters would be hearing, singing, dancing to, what they remember. Or it was until my seventeen-year-old grandson got a portable radio and sleeps with it on. Music is not only part of the environment which your characters react to, but may develop character. Certainly it will indicate character to your reader. A girl who by choice puts on a Gieseking record of a Beethoven sonata and one who puts on Copland's "El Salón México" and another who prefers Bill Haley's "Rock around the Clock" have to be different, neither better nor worse, but different.

Food has character indications, too. I can't imagine why, but I remember whole a line from Elizabeth Bowen's The Last September which read, "It still surprised her that Laurence, who looked ethereal, should spend so much time when he was not being intellectual in talking and apparently thinking about food. She supposed that this was because he had, as he had once said, no emotional life." I expect I remember it because it is so true and I intend to use it sometime when I need it. Not the words—the thought. Lack of an emotional life is one reason teen-agers have such odd appetites. I remember, too, how magnificently Edna Ferber used food in one of my favorite-of-all-time short stories, "The Afternoon of a Faun."

You know much more about the faun, who is a young mechanic, because of how and what he eats.

It is an indication, too, of background. Of how a character was brought up and where and in what kind of a home.

These are reporting jobs which every writer must do all the time, sometimes specifically, sometimes in general. Not only for the accuracy of his own knowledge, but to keep his interest and excitement in life around him at a high boiling point all the time. I once asked Fulton Oursler why he never drank and he said, "I was born drunk. I was born intoxicated with life, all of it. So were you. Add alcohol to this and it's a conflagration." This is true, and the high emotional reaction is an absolute essential. All writers have it. Nor must you be fooled by, say, the man-of-the-world poise and savoir-faire of a Gallico, he is actually an old softie. Or the cold, dead-pan exterior Ring Lardner presented to the world. Inside, Ring was a man of the violence against evil which produced "Champion" and "Hair Cut."

Fury against is as fine and strong a motivation as love of or for—it is actually but another face of the same thing, as Jesus' driving the money-changers from the temple came from the same love of God and man as healing the lepers or casting out demons.

Most writers are iconoclasts in some way or another. Bitter against existing wrongs. Often in history it has been their role to stir up the public about existing wrongs and to inflame and inspire them to act to correct those wrongs. I remember when

I said to President Franklin Roosevelt that I was in Washington getting background for some fiction stories and that it would not interest him, he answered, with a smile, "Remember *Uncle Tom's Cabin?* That was fiction the President of the United States should have been interested in. It's been called the book that started the War between the States. Dickens gave his government a lot of trouble about debtors' prisons and almshouses and courts of chancery."

It seems to me that laziness, inertia prevent writers from doing the proper reporting on fiction stories rather than the excuses of high-brow artistry which some of them give me. Unless you are writing *Alice in Wonderland*, or *The Wizard of Oz*, also a grown-up classic if you read it right, or *Gulliver's Travels*, you are working from life as definitely as does a painter. It's silly to pretend anything else, and if that is what is meant by the use of the word "creative," it's phony. Each writer will give a new, a more humorous, a more tragic or fantastic, a lighter or some serious interpretation of the thing seen, he will select the character of whom he wishes to paint a portrait, and obviously the grandfather of Thurber will be different from the grandfather of Chekhov, but there was a grandfather in life to begin with.

All good and great writers recognize the need. For the fiction writer may not ask for that suspension of belief which is granted to the teller of fairy tales, or the fantasy method under which Swift put forth the biting political and social satire of Gulliver. Thus the short story writer must always be believed, what he writes must be entirely possible and probable to the reader, his characters must live so that the reader recognizes them as human beings whether he has ever happened to meet them or not.

Some of this is contributed by careful reporting. It takes time and effort and is perhaps one of the reasons why newspaper reporting has, on the whole, been the best training for successful short story writers. Once I had an idea for a story about the reopening of the Golden Gate at the beginning of the second world war. I stayed a month in San Francisco, getting the facts, and I interviewed over twenty men before a young man named Bechtel, head of a big shipbuilding company, gave me in one sentence the essential story on which I could operate and in which my character could move. I still remember the sentence. He said, "One reason I'm building ships is because that was one of my crews on Midway."

If you wish to study a fine job of reporting, reread Lardner's "The Golden Honeymoon," one of the finest short stories of this century. Ring spent a lot of time in Florida, but not in the locality of this story. One hundred per cent a story of characters, the characters are made realer than most by the power of the factual reporting. The horseshoe pitching, for instance. And as an example of vocabulary, let me give you a line where the golden honeymooner who tells the story reports to us how he and Mother made up a row. "So I put my arm around her shoulder and she stroked my hand and I guess we got kind of spoony." I defy anyone to find another word as fitting there as "spoony."

Writing is an art. It must begin to dawn on you that it is also work. Work. Not just behind the typewriter or pen. All the time. I love it. It's the most exciting and wonderful work there is. But it's work.

Memory.

I wish I could write that word here in letters of fire nine feet high, like a sign in Times Square.

In my reporting days I interviewed many of the leading figures of our world. If I had to pick one characteristic they had in common, it would be a good memory.

I do not mean a memory like the professor's, or even the actor's. A writer's memory is different from all others. Unconscious, subconscious, subliminal, the heart's core, the innermost recess of the mind, a tape recorder, a wax disc, a filing system, and it never, never, never stops. This is a gift, an intrinsic part, an inborn trait of nature, an essential of the inwardness without which I myself would hesitate to encourage anyone to try to become a short story writer. A professional short story writer.

One of my boys, who is a lawyer, may sometime make a fine writer. I told this to a friend, and she said, "Oh—he can write, can he?" and I said, "Well, I wouldn't know about that, but I suppose he can learn like the rest of us. But he was born with a writer's memory. He remembers the right things, the things that prove character, the unusual circumstances, and he re-members them at the right time."

It is a gift, but I also know that once you are made aware of it and of its vital consequence, it is possible to begin to stimu-late it, turn it on, keep it on, see that it registers, emphasize its recordings for a time until it becomes automatic, as it should and must be.

Once at a dinner party I watched Olivia De Haviland sitting very quietly in the drawing room and I thought how intent her great dark eyes were, how they watched everybody. A brilliant newspaperwoman was telling a story of a trial she had covered, with gestures, and I saw that Olivia was quietly making those same gestures with her hands. Once she asked a question. "What did the girl do with her hands while she was on the stand?" And when the reporter told her, Olivia made that gesture, that strange, stiff, paralyzed gesture, too. This was the actress's memory at work, recording for some future use. I have seen Helen Hayes do it, too. And Judy Garland.

All from life, life, life.

Don't you see? It is all from life, and your memory is your recorder of dialogue, of gestures, of incidents, of business day after day. A professional writer could not possibly make them all up even if that were the way to do it, which it isn't. You do not photograph. You sketch them all deep into your memory tape. There, in the amazing creation of your mind or soul, is some process, some electric arm that, when you need this in a story you are writing—whether you are plotting it in your head or putting it down on paper—reaches in and pulls it out and comes up with it for your use.

I have a remarkable ear memory. This is partly due to Mr. William Randolph Hearst, who told me to cultivate this when I was a very young reporter. To concentrate on it. I once covered a press conference given by the Prime Minister of England, then Ramsay MacDonald, and due to an afternoon paper deadline had to come up with my story before we received the stenographer record of what he'd said from City News Service. In my quotes I had three words wrong. This experience has been invaluable to me as a short story writer. Trade vocabularies, things people actually say, sports jargon, which is the universal language that all Americans understand, witty sentences—these stick in my ear and, interpreted, changed to fit the occasion perhaps, are more useful than I can tell you.

To show you that this all works automatically in time:

The telegram announcing that His Majesty's Government regretted to inform me that Pilot Officer William St. Johns had been killed in action found me sitting quietly in the riverside living room of my house in Beekman Place. Naturally, I didn't know what I said or did. No matter how long it has hung over you, you never expect death. Later as a writer I had to wonder what I had said and I asked the inner memory and it played it back to me. "No no no no no no no——NO NO. No. Not Bill. No no——"

The other day here at the inn, the husband in a wonderful couple who occupied the other suite in my bungalow under the orange trees was taken to the hospital with a heart attack. Half an hour later his wife came back, and as I went to her, seeing her face, she said, "It's all over. It can't be all over so quick. It's—all over. So quick."

This I have to record.

This is knowledge of human nature. Her sorrow was great and real. They had been married many years and, as I had seen, were gaily devoted. Her first reaction was utter bewilderment at how quickly we can move from life to death. Alive one instant—dead the next. Also, of course, her soul was using it to protect her from the first shock, to let it come by degrees that her husband was dead.

All your knowledge of human nature records as memory. When you start to plot, that memory works. If you are not deeply, constantly, always interested in human beings, don't attempt to be a writer. You don't have to like them all. But you have to be interested in them all. Then you will take in and keep the memory of what they do. Say. How they look. You will know what to do about your character who is a woman whose greed destroys her marriage because you remember Susie or Daisy and how she always went around behind you turning off the electric lights. Or a man you knew who was always running out of gas because he hated to buy it.

Naturally, experience helps in all this. The years give you rich stocks, from which you clip coupons. But it is also true, I sincerely believe, that the childhood record is deeply engraved and very clear. Children are more impressed by what they see and hear, by the people they know, their confines are narrower, therefore they have a file cabinet of memories, too.

I went at one time quite often with Damon and Pat Runyon to a restaurant on Broadway called Lindy's, which became Mindy's in *Guys and Dolls*. It was Damon's favorite spot. I remember how Rothstein, the gambler, used to come in late at night and how he always had a corner table where no one could come up behind him—or even approach him from the side. I know how Damon used that and many, many other things he saw and remembered from those days in stories he wrote years later.

A great newspaperman who had a weakness for illiterate and violent women once had a girl who ran off with a gangster. He was heartbroken, and when I went by to see him and asked if there was anything I could do—people hurt just as much and sometimes more, you know, when they know the whole thing's their own fault—he said, "Yes. Get her clothes out of here, will you? I can't stand them. The smell of them. That's the worst." I remembered that when I needed something in the story "Maid, Wife nor Widow." Then my girl's husband had gone to jail for ten years. I needed it.

In "The First Temptation," the opening story in the series for Jack O'Connell which I did for *Cosmopolitan*, there is a deathbed scene I'm a little proud of. Again, see the wondrous process of this inward working. This is a story about a will contest. For the woman who made the will I used the grandmother of a dear friend of my convent days at Notre Dame in

San Jose, although, as we always do, I changed her a great deal and in my story she wasn't a grandmother at all but an old maid. She was one of the picturesque early Spanish California aristocratic beauties—I remembered her driving through the streets of Santa Barbara in an open victoria with four white horses and a postilion, a mantilla over her black hair. I couldn't have been more than ten at the time, but I remembered her well. I also remembered well an early scene in Kathleen Norris' *Certain People of Importance*, a fine historical record of old ladies in early California. What I didn't realize as I put these together to get my character of the lady who made the will—why I used this Spanish California character instead of a rich old woman I knew on Nob Hill or a society leader in Chicago or my friend Evalyn Walsh McLean in Washington—was that I wanted the deathbed scene from a story my daughter, Elaine St. Johns, covered when she was on the Los Angeles *Mirror*. In a cave down on the banks of the Los Angeles River. For this, the lady had to be Spanish Californian.

This is plotting.

A lot of it takes place inside as you brood. It goes round and round and comes out *there.*

To observe it in the story of a young writer, take that brilliant short story genius—I use the word genius advisedly—William Saroyan. Take *The Daring Young Man on the Flying Trapeze.* Or *My Name Is Aram.* How all the stories of his childhood come welling up from his memory and his knowledge. There the use of a song—of music—is the great device.

Perfection. I have a feeling that having written out his great spontaneity, Mr. Saroyan is now learning the technique that will bring him back in an even more solid greatness. Usually great stories—the classic stories—come from a writer who has already through years acquired the blending. Saroyan hit the jackpot the first time. Very rare, that is.

Which brings us to instinct or invention or intuition, of which Mr. Saroyan obviously had so much.

Nobody can teach you that, or even tell you what it is or much about it. Except this:

Goethe said once that we build character in the stream of the world but talent in solitude.

After the bustle of reporting and observation and living, it is well to go into solitude. To withdraw. Into an attic, a place beside the sea, an alp, anywhere you can be alone. Where all these things that you have observed, all the people you have loved or despised or wished to drive from the temple, all you have heard, all the songs you have sung and the dances you have danced may have time to become your own. Where your mind and your soul may, in seclusion, have time to function.

If they do, then you may be a very good or even a great storyteller.

If they don't, you may still be a successful storyteller but you will always be in the second or third class.

For invention, inspiration, intuition come from the Source, which every writer knows exists. All any of us can do is be still sometimes and see if we can hear what it says to us.

12.

I would like to sum up here the few things I have found it possible to say honestly about the technique of writing a short story. There are not many, but I believe those I do know are sound.

Spend most of your time before you start to write, in the sense of putting anything except notes down on paper.

Know your characters well. *Know* them. In the same way that Kipling made me as sure as I was at nine and still am that Mowgli was real, as sure as Mary Roberts Rinehart made Tish part of my acquaintance, or Steinbeck made me know Jody, you must know your characters before you start. Live with them. Pay no attention to what other people think of you as you blithely or gloomily inhabit a world where you converse with and watch these people you are painting from life—putting together. Live with them until one day you hear yourself laugh out loud at something one of them said to you or find you have to wipe away a real tear because one of them said to you, "It's—all over. So *quick*." Then you can begin to plot.

Plotting, then, is working out those things

which could and would happen to a particular character or characters. This is a combination of reporting, memory, and invention. But you have to do it.

Always have your ending clear from the beginning.

This most vital technical point in any short story is where you start it. Spend any amount of time needed to measure this one. In the end it will be time saved.

Stick to the point.

One minor story maybe, interwoven to prove a point. No more.

One of the most troublesome problems with stories new writers bring me is that they have two or three stories in one story. Their fear always seems to be that they haven't enough story. The mess that results is dreadful.

One of the best writers I ever knew at a time when he was forming his talent was a reporter who used to work with me on the New York *Journal-American* named Syd Boehm. Like all newspapermen, he knew a great deal about human nature and how it behaved in the raw, his mind was a storehouse of characters and happenings and he could write like Runyon. But I had to go off by myself and have hysterics over the first yarn he brought me when he decided—as many reporters do, but all too many never get any further—to try fiction. It had exactly *four* entire stories in it. As a result, of course, none of them was any good. Hollywood stole Syd almost at once— you have seen his name on *The Tall Men* and a dozen other hit pictures of late—which is probably where his great wealth of inventive talent and full storehouse belong. But—I've always been rather sorry because he had the makings of a fine short story writer. He's now under contract to 20th Century-Fox and he's still very young, so maybe someday he'll retire from the screen and write short stories.

There should be one story, plus a minor plot. No more. For the reader will wish to follow your character closely. If it's a fine character to love or hate there is hardly enough time as it is. Stick to the point. Keep the reader's interest focused on that character. See how Edna Ferber does it in "Gay Old Dog," a great tour de force if there ever was one.

Work with a Thesaurus on either hand. Vocabulary. Never be satisfied until you have found the one word that entirely expresses the thing inside which you know and are trying to say.

Find someone who cares—who will listen—to explore an idea with if you can and maybe to read your second—or third—or whatever draft comes up that you feel anybody could read. Personally I never know—sometimes it's the second. It has been the fourteenth. I have been very fortunate, aside from some of the great editors I've worked with, in having my daughter Elaine, who since she was in her teens has been my best friend and severest critic. She has a cold, merciless editorial mind. No amount of horsing around or explaining will alter the fact that I haven't said what I intended to say so that she, the reader, got it. Or that I haven't created a character in whom she believes—or one she likes—or will read on to see if she gets her comeuppance or anything else. In many years I have not mailed a story until it suited her and she has been wrong only once. One story she was really crazy about didn't suit the editor—and it has taken me two years to know why. I am about to do it over—and it will be a better story. I used the main feminine character to express my detestation of a certain kind of woman, a detestation Elaine shares. She wasn't real. She was a marionette saying in a very squeaky voice the things I had always wanted to say about women who destroy their husband's happiness and the peace of their marriage because they insist they could have had a career, when everybody knows they had no more talent than an unborn rabbit and less guts and stamina. I do not write well when I don't like my character. Some writers do but I don't. On the whole, I have found the men and women, young and old, whom I have known to be basically brave and good, always trying to find more light, filled so often with kindness and willingness to help others. They have had faults, few greater than my own it seems to me, considering the advantages I have had, and where would we be for stories if they didn't? So I have had to find for my story a woman for whom I can feel compassion, and this I have finally done, and one of these days I will try it again.

You may find the outlet you need for discussing stories and going over them when they are in shape in your family, as I did with my daughter. Or among yourselves as a group, as it used to be in Greenwich Village and the little cafés in Paris and years ago in certain sections in London. I have seen this happen sometimes in New York and occasionally among groups I've known at school. That should be the purpose of manuscript clubs and literary societies, and I wish they would do more of it. But in my experience all too often they simply meet to listen to someone like me tell them what can be told in a brief and necessarily very general hour's talk. They would accomplish much more if they fought and argued and talked far into the night and tore each other's work to pieces and helped put it back together again. Of course the professors in creative writing courses or in some of the writing teaching circles, the good ones, can do more than anyone else, and even the bad ones keep their students writing and there is someone to talk to. There is activity.

Face the fact immediately that writing means long, hard, backbreaking hours at the typewriter or desk. Some of them hours of joy beyond description, of course. But also some of them pure unadulterated grind. Margaret Cousins, one of the most sensitive and charming writers in this country today, is a big, handsome Texan, with that combination of laughter and tears which comes through all her stories. Last time I sat with her for hours over a chop at Michael's pub in New York we decided it was the greatest life in the world if you didn't weaken. If you lived through it.

Talent makes it easier, and I would say that the majority of successful professional writers had some story talent to begin with. But not all. A number of writers didn't have it.

But they were impelled by a strong inner urge which took its place.

The things that are most devotedly to be wished for are:

A nose for a story. Without that—oh dear!

A writer's memory.

A great, abiding, never failing interest in people.

A set of quick and violent reactions to things and people.

A real stamina, not an ability to endure discipline but to build *self-discipline*, so that you can wrap it up.

Without these it would be better not to try to learn the things that anybody can learn. Like writing, and vocabulary, and plotting and such.

Work is essential. Study is, in my opinion, necessary.

It has always puzzled me a little that people think they can just write. I know of no other profession or trade where some initial study and practice and apprenticeship are not regarded as requisite, inescapable, inevitable, and even compulsory. The singer must learn to sing, the composer must study the laws of harmony, the actor goes to summer stock, vaudeville, or on the road—and we had better actors when more time was spent at this, there are few such artists as Helen Hayes or Katharine Cornell or Charles Laughton who have not served a term of practice. The violinist spends a lifetime, beginning in childhood and continuing. I shall never forget spending a few days with Jascha Heifetz and his wife and realizing that even then, when he was acknowledged the greatest artist in the world in his field, he worked four and five hours a day with his accompanist. Doctors—lawyers—painters—all work to learn their trade.

But I have met very few people who didn't think they could write a good book if they just had the time.

Every man knows his own business plus writing.

What they mean, of course, is that their life is an interesting story, or they have observed in their lives things that would make interesting stories, and this is completely true. But it isn't all or enough.

I am also amazed at how easily discouraged the young folks are today. If they receive a couple of rejections they are a little too inclined to say, "Ah—that proves what I've always thought, they don't really want good stories," or, "I guess I haven't any talent." They have not yet learned their scales or practiced more than a few pieces. They must not be so ready to give up. Maupassant, under the guidance and tutelage of Flaubert, wrote a hundred short stories before one was submitted for sale. His complete works amounted to over two hundred short stories, and the majority of them are good and they became classics and he the founder, really, of the modern school.

If you are willing to study the works of the masters you will improve and learn. I know this, I have seen it. What can they teach us specifically? Let us take one or two direct examples to answer this question and show how fine stories can be used.

What, for instance, did I myself learn from Damon Runyon's stories?

Ah, he had a great trick—a great method.

Because of his hard-boiled style, his hard-boiled characters, names, places, dialogue, my blessed and beloved Damon wrote some of the most sentimental, almost maudlin tales ever put down on paper. As far as the actual plot, the actual what-happened, these are dillies. Examine a couple of Runyon stories. In "Butch Minds the Baby" a safe-cracker takes his baby with him on a job and Damon proves that he cares more whether the baby gets his bottle than whether he gets the money in the safe. No matter how tough or even bad a man may be, he loves babies. "The Lily of St. Pierre," my own favorite, "Madame la Gimp," which became that successful movie *Lady for a Day*, "The Brain Goes Home," with the raggedy doll who brought the flowers out of the ash can to lay on his coffin: "Gentlemen, the King!"—I'm ashamed to tell you. You do some of the work about now. Read these yourself and break them down into fifty-word synopses. This'll teach you!

And remember these are great and very successful short stories.

So from Runyon you know that if you want to write a very sentimental story, tell it about hard-boiled people, and select hard-boiled language to express the sentimental sentiments.

Maugham's slightly dry, sometimes rather formal, very British underplaying helps to make real the South Seas and spy stories, which of themselves are often flamboyant, exotic, unusual—so if your story is very colorful and adventurous and might be unbelievable or implausible, a quiet style will help it.

Note the utter simplicity of Conan Doyle's method in setting up the famous Sherlock Holmes. His style is open and aboveboard, artless, almost naïve, as is the storyteller, the good Dr. Watson. You see Sherlock Holmes through his eyes and they become your own. This is a—"trick" is a word that has the wrong connotation—this is a technique, a way, a skill, as it were.

Some techniques fit one kind of story, some another. It is only fair and it seems to me highly intelligent to discover the best method of telling the story you have in mind and then employing it.

I am often asked if there are taboos. I don't know any if the story is good enough, except to remember you're not writing on fences. Common decencies should be preserved—on the whole.

I also think it is wise, if possible, to establish work hours. You can, of course, work any time anyplace if necessary. We all have. But I think regular work hours establish a continuity in your own consciousness that is valuable. I myself work from five in the morning until twelve, or as long as I can or want to. I like this shift now because I wake up refreshed and the morning is a lovely time and you get into it before there can be telephone calls. But it doesn't matter. I used to work from after the kids went to bed until dawn. Any shift you like—but it helps, as I say, to make it the same one every day.

13.

I would like to end this book, which I find could go on and on forever—like talking shop all night with Gallico or Maggie Cousins or Syd Boehm or Fulton Oursler —by telling the story of what happened to cause me to write it at all.

This story will also prove the last point I want to emphasize and perhaps reiterate.

Work with what you have at hand and find stories where you are, about situations you know, around characters with whom you are familiar.

April Oursler Armstrong is the daughter of the late Fulton Oursler, author of *The Greatest Story Ever Told*, and his wife Grace, a fine writer herself and a woman for whom I can find no sufficiently worthy adjectives. Fulton never could either, and he spent years trying, so I'll let it go.

I have loved April since she was a youngster running around up at the Oursler Cape Cod home in Falmouth, a place of cherished memories for me and for every other writer who ever was lucky enough to go there on a visit. Of course she grew up—they will do it —all of a sudden in about five minutes there she was, graduating from Bryn Mawr, marrying a rugged young assistant district attorney in New York, having babies, being her father's right-hand collaborator, and becoming a writer on her own.

Fulton's sudden and unexpected death left his family and friends bereft 'way beyond common. There just didn't seem to be anybody to replace him. One thing it was good to know, April was in a position, having been working with him, to finish the trilogy with *The Greatest Faith Ever Known*, which she did in a way that must have made her father very proud of her wherever he was when he read it.

Then came her simple, heart-moving *Fátima: Pilgrimage to Peace*, which even someone like me with a Methodist grand-father could love and respect.

One evening I was having dinner with April and her hus-band, Martin Armstrong, who coauthored the *Pilgrimage*, and the three young Armstrongs, and to tell you the truth a very-much-about-to-be fourth one, and I was saying to April that I had liked the book very much and that she was growing in grace and ability, and suddenly she said, "Yes. I'm glad you feel that way and I hope it's true. But I still can't write a short story."

I said, "Oh nonsense!"

She shook her head and said. "No. I just can't. I want to very much. I think you can say so much you want to say in short stories that you can't say anywhere else. But I've tried and I've tried and I can't bring it off. Ever since that time you remember when you made me start reading Kipling, I've tried. I still can't."

This distressed me. I couldn't understand it. I think short stories are so much easier to write than articles. I hate being bound by facts.

"Another thing," April said, "short stories you can write at home and it does look as if I'm going to have a big family and I won't always be able to go off to Fátima, will I?"

So I said, "Look, I'm going back to California day after tomorrow, but if you can come down to my hotel tomorrow morning—I'm tied up all afternoon and your brother Tony is getting married the following morning and I leave on the Super Chief that afternoon—maybe I can help you. Anybody who can write as well as you can and knows as much about people as you must have learned from your father and mother has to be able to write a short story."

Turned out a really gray morning, raining and blowing, but we holed up in my quiet suite at the San Carlos, which is a hotel in the East Fifties where they understand about writers, and started to try to find what block was bothering April and the short stories.

It wasn't long before I understood her trouble. She didn't know what a short story was. She hadn't accepted it as simply a story that entertains readers and can be told completely in few enough words so a magazine can publish it. In her mind was some exalted, unfamiliar concept, 'way off up in the sky, different, strange, something if possible she didn't know anything about. One thing it couldn't be was something right under her nose.

We worked awhile, hammering away, and then I ordered some coffee so we could stretch our mental muscles, and she began to glow with joy again over the new house they had just bought up in Connecticut.

"Isn't it too wonderful?" she said. "Of course it's an answer to a prayer. We just love it, and we had to find a house in the country—with four children and probably more we couldn't stay in a New York apartment, but you know how it is, for what we could pay down we didn't know whether we'd ever find—and at first it just didn't seem as though this—I cried coming home the first time and then——"

I won't tell the rest here because it would spoil the story.

It was something that might happen to any couple, with children, trying to buy a house with only so much cash to put down, from, as she told it, another young couple who——

Anyhow, when she finished, I said, "That's a wonderful short story. You going to write it, or shall I?"

She stared at me with utter complete disbelief and bewilderment.

"But——" she said finally.

"That," I said, "is a short story. A fine one. It is about people I am going to like very much. It is about something that everybody is interested in—a home, getting a home. It has a lovely twist because the villains turn out to be in exactly the same fix as the people we love and want to see get what they desire, so we end in laughter and tears. There is nothing about this story with which you are not familiar. You know the New York apartment you want to get out of—and your husband— and how you hunted and hunted and were discouraged and finally found your dream house and then broke your hearts because it didn't seem—and there is that wonderful scene in the living room you have fallen in love with—you and Martin at once—and the young couple who built the house to sell at the other——" Suddenly, much as I love her, and she's like a daughter to me, I yelled at her. I do sometimes. I said, "What more do you want?"

She said slowly, "I never thought of it that way—I guess it was too close—it didn't seem as if it could be a story, just something happening every day——"

"You write it or I will," I said, trying to sound as much like a marine top kick as I could. Or a city editor.

At Tony's wedding reception the next day April and Martin and I shared a table in the Sherry-Netherland with Joe Marks of Doubleday, who was Fulton's publisher and is now April's and mine, so that it was quite a family gathering. April, who didn't know then that the new baby boy was to be born that afternoon and was probably feeling the exuberance that builds up to birth—you know how you always want to wash and iron and clean bureau drawers—told him I had taught her more about short story writing in a morning than she'd ever dreamed of before and that now she was going to be able to do it.

Whereupon Joe Marks said maybe I ought to write a book

called *How to Write a Story and Sell It*, and I said if April sold her story maybe I would.

A few weeks later I received a wire saying *Good Housekeeping* had bought April's story.

So—here is the book.

It seems to me I have stressed and belabored the things that are vital to me and that I have not seen in other books about short stories, probably because most of them are written by teachers and experts and not by those who are professional writers.

There is one last word. Always, always, always give it everything you've got. Otherwise, it's not worth doing. Reach, and every time reach for the moon. Try with all your heart to write a great story.

And remember what it says in a sampler I had a friend work for me and hang over my desk.

It is what George Ade's mother once said to somebody who was raving about George Ade's great short stories. "Anybody," she said, "can write as well as George does, but George does."

And now I want you to read the short story April wrote and sold because I said the same things to her I've said here, so that may prove maybe I know what I'm talking about.

For once.

THE

HOUSE

ON

SWEETFERN

ROAD

BY

APRIL

OURSLER

ARMSTRONG

The house stood in the middle of an acre of bulldozed mud, clumps of birch trees and wild laurel, and piles of concrete blocks and unlaid flagstones. Across the front, along Sweetfern Road, was a stone wall, green with the lichen and moss of a hundred years. A freshly laid driveway stretched straight and clean to the other road bounding the corner lot. The house was white, with gray shutters. Rain slid off the roof, gurgled in the gutters, and splattered through the holes where the drainpipes would soon be placed. Atop the garage cupola, the weather vane swayed gently in the November breeze.

At one end of the stone wall, near the cluster of R.F.D. mailboxes, stood a sign: "FOR SALE. TEL. ST. 7-5273."

Saturday, at five thirty, Mrs. Peabody met her friend Mrs. Stevens for tea and a chance to compare notes about their married daughters.

"How Cathy manages is beyond me," Mrs. Peabody said. "Her fourth baby due any day, and there they all are in that tiny apartment. Only two bedrooms, mind you, and tricycles and Teddy bears everywhere, and the noise——"

"They can't find a place?" asked Mrs. Stevens, thinking of her own daughter's suave apartment, so soon to be cluttered with a first baby's impediments. "You just wish you could find it for them, fix everything up for them the way you could when they were little, don't you? *I* do. Yet I dread interfering. Isn't it awful to be both a mother *and* a mother-in-law?"

Behind her rhinestoned glasses, Mrs. Peabody's eyes were solemn. "It is. Awful. Cathy and Jim have skimped for seven years, ever since they were married, to get a really nice house, big enough for the family they want to raise. They've saved eight thousand dollars for a down payment. And still they can't find what they want. Wish they'd let me help them. Maybe for a bit more money——"

"Like my kids. So independent you could shake them. Yet I love them for it."

Mrs. Peabody nodded. "Is there anything lonelier than wanting to help someone and not being let? Or than knowing that the little girl you love is a woman? This is Cathy's fourth child. I had only one."

Across town at suppertime, in a room overlooking Riverside Drive, Mrs. Sargent sat alone with her canaries and her coffee. Below her, traffic blared and snarled in the rain. The birds twittered. But she heard only her own voice, sorting her thoughts aloud. Ever since Mr. Sargent died, she had feared silence.

"I've figured and figured, and there's no answer. They want a house, but they want more than they'll ever find, even at that price." She humphed at the birds. "When I was young, eight or nine thousand bought a fine house. Now it's hardly a down payment. Better they save their money and not buy."

She sipped the coffee. "They could try another apartment. Living's easier than in a house. But there are no apartments for their pocketbook with room for children. They're right about that."

She folded her napkin into a fan shape. "Even a project or a development won't do. They're for beginning families, not for four kids. And remodeling an old house sounds good, but it usually ends up costing more than buying a new one. Guess I ought to tell them they've set their sights too high. They're looking for a house to fall in love with—and they should just take what they can get. But I won't tell them that."

Her thoughts darted back to the year her baby Jim had been born (her baby who now had a wife and nearly four babies of his own). Her Jim's first bed had been carved mahogany, ruffled with organdy, and he had had a room of his own, with sunlight streaming in, and a little Irish girl to rock him and make his beef broth.

"Ah, the poor kids," said Mrs. Sargent. "They're making good money, more than we ever had, and they get less for it. It's a bad world where it's so hard to get the simple things like a house."

At quarter to nine that night Mrs. Sargent's boy, Jim, who

was thirty-three and graying over the ears, sat beside Mrs. Peabody's little girl, Cathy, who was twenty-eight and who, in her ninth month, looked as if she were trying to smuggle a Thanksgiving pumpkin out of the market.

Jim had brought the early copies of the Sunday papers. Cathy had cleared spacemen and rocket ships off the coffee table, moved the stuffed dog and the monkey from the love seat, and spread the real-estate section out before them. From long habit they were equipped with pencils, scissors, filing cards, cellophane tape, and sets of mental maps and commuters' timetables—and hope.

Cathy wiggled her toes in her red slippers and kissed Jim under his ear. His collar was still damp from the rain. "This time it'll be waiting for us. Tonight we find it."

Jim grinned. "Mm-hm. Ten rooms and ten acres, brand-new, for three thousand. Or should it have a swimming pool too?"

Jim's thick black pencil moved down the columns of tiny print to the major heading "HOUSES—CONNECTICUT."

"We're sure it has to be Connecticut?" he asked, as he had asked each weekend for the past three months.

Dutifully Cathy considered the question as if it were new, which it was not, and important, which it was.

"We have to stay within commuting distance of New York. From March through June we looked at Long Island. New Jersey we looked at too, but that's out because your office is on the east side of the city, and that makes commuting really tough. We looked at Westchester—and its taxes. And in those four months we never saw one house we fell in love with."

"And we like Connecticut," Jim added solemnly.

"Yes." In the instant's silence they pictured the open countryside, the trees and winding roads and stone walls and rushing brooks they yearned to make their own.

"And we're agreed that I'll not spend more than an hour each way on the train?"

Cathy nodded, and a black curl slid down her forehead. "There are only four towns we want to look at—Greenwich, Darien, New Canaan, and Stamford."

Jim's lips tightened in agreement. He whistled as he bent over the paper. His pencil slashed through all the ads from towns out of commuting range, through enticing offers at low prices from Bethel and Brookfield, Candlewood Lake, Danbury, Sharon, Weston, and Westport. More slowly he X-ed out the houses that were priced too high, and the discreet snares where no price was named.

Sixteen ads remained. Together they read them, silently clothing the strange abbreviations with pictures, visualizing the bdrms and cls, liv rms and liv-din rms, the firepls, the ½ acs and acs, the remod Cols, the lg rchs, the oil h w ht, the prchs and gars. With conscious effort they whittled away the non-essentials, discarding such words as "luxurious," "extraordinary," "homey," and "must be seen to be appreciated," concentrating only on what was specifically stated—and more important, what was not stated.

"This says 'Darien commuting.' Remember we learned that means it's not *in* Darien. Could be ten miles away."

"This one—no mention of cellar, or attic, or garage. Where would you store anything?"

"This one's so emphatic about being convenient to schools and shopping, it's probably on a tiny plot just off Main Street. Or near the depot."

They were left with six ads, carefully clipped and taped to file cards.

"We'll go look at them tomorrow. Maybe one will be ours."

Cathy nodded. How often they had said that! How often she had driven up in the middle of the week to track down a promising lead from the daily paper, the boys in the back seat and the baby beside her in front. Why, oh why couldn't an ad come out and warn you what was wrong with a house? There was the one she dashed out in the rain to see, a beautiful house —with a front yard that ended in a 30-foot drop to the new truck highway. There was the one built in a gully, where after a three-week dry spell the ground was still swampy. And the one where two of the four bedrooms actually measured only 7′ x 7′ each.

Her eyes traveled over her living room, seeing it as a stranger might. The tattered upholstery on the chairs where the boys played house and stagecoach and pirates (where else were they to play on rainy days?). The tricycles parked by the television set. The Indian village under the piano. The soot-stained curtains, washed only three weeks before, hanging at the windows where no sunlight ever entered. "If only I didn't want so much," said Cathy, controlling her voice to a monotone. "I want a place where the children can run, and feel God's sun and air instead of soot and Central Park. A place where we can each grow as a person, with a little privacy. A place to keep things—where I can keep baby clothes for a new generation and start an heirloom or two. Where you can have a darkroom and a vegetable patch, and the boys can——" Her voice snapped over the ache in her throat. "So many, many people have homes. Is it so much to ask?"

Jim looked away quickly, as he always did when she was about to cry. "You used to say home is where we are. That where love is and God is, there is home." He rolled up his sleeves, paying great attention to each fold. "We'll look again, and we'll find it. I promise you."

"I'm sick of looking. I've had it. And I know darn well that millions of people are worse off than us. People living all in one room, with cold water. People living with their in-laws. So don't tell me about that. Maybe we should give up looking."

The light from the living room flooded the bedroom, onto Deirdre's crib. The old floors creaked as Cathy tiptoed past the packing boxes that held the baby-to-come's crib and mattress. She stepped on a hard-rubber lump on the floor, and Deirdre's doll squawked in protest. The crib rattled. Deirdre flung herself over on her back, whimpered, then howled.

Cathy stood still. "All I want is to go into my own bedroom

just once and be able to turn on all the lights and be alone. We've never had a room to ourselves since the first baby," she whispered through her tears. "Just to be alone for ten minutes somewhere. I'm never even left alone in the bathtub without an audience."

She turned on the light. Little Deirdre of the snub nose and the blue eyes looked like a rain-drenched will-o'-the-wisp, all pucker-faced and forlorn. Cathy swept her into her arms and reached for a diaper.

The pile of diapers on the shelf under the baby bath unbalanced itself and fell, sprawling and heaping, across the doorway. Cathy looked at them and sighed. The floor was so much farther away these last couple of weeks.

Dierdre was staring at her gravely, and Cathy, looking at those baby eyes, suddenly remembered the picture of a guardian angel that had hung over her bed years before. Clutching the baby to her, she found herself praying that prayer that was still her gateway to each night's sleep: "Angel of God, my guardian dear, to whom His love commits me here, Night and day be at my side, to light and guard and rule and guide."

She picked up the diapers, changed Deirdre, and led her out to the living room.

"Jim," said Cathy, "we've got to believe that the right place is waiting for us somewhere. We can't get discouraged. Jim, we've got to keep hold of our dreams."

His eyes brightened as he saw her smile. "Even if the dream isn't practical? Doesn't make sense?"

"Just because we haven't found it yet doesn't prove our house doesn't exist—at our price. Innocent till proved guilty, my dear Mr. Attorney."

Jim let Deirdre try her new molars on his thumb knuckle. "Guess we'll go look some more tomorrow, huh, little girl?"

Out at the big white house on Sweetfern Road that same Saturday night, unshaded work lights glared bleakly in the faces of another young man and his wife, still building a dream. Nine months ago they had started construction of this house. Now they were nearly through. The strain and hope of those months were written on their faces and in the set of their shoulders.

Now in the white plastered living room, Barbara Bennett was scraping stickers off the panes of glass in the windows. Fred Bennett sat on the hall staircase in his fatigue pants and sweat shirt, notebook and chewed green pencil in his hands.

"We'll never ever get thirty-four thousand for it now," he said. "November's here, and people don't buy houses on rainy weekends. If only that mason and that so-and-so of a plasterer —"

"We lost two months because of them," said Barbara grimly, sponging a pane of glass. "Two of the best selling months."

"And two months of our own mortgage payments on the deal. Barbara, we can't carry this through the winter. It'd be different if we were big operators, but this is cutting it awful close."

"We'd get more for it in the spring."

"But we'd have to heat it, pay taxes on it—and go on paying interest on our mortgage. And our creditors are starting to howl. The well digger called me, and the heating contractor. Barbara, we'd lose more than a thousand waiting till spring. Our capital would be tied up. We couldn't do a thing. We've got to sell now. Guess our only hope is someone transferred to this area by a big company, someone who needs a house desperately."

"What do you think we could get?"

"In the spring, thirty-four or thirty-five. Now? Thirty. Maybe less."

"Probably less." Barbara put down the scraper and walked over to the fireplace. She stood on the stones of the hearth, rocking slowly back and forth, and her face was pale. "Twenty-nine would mean about three thousand dollars profit. After nine months of work and worry, and all the plans before that. Sometimes I wonder whether it's worth it. That's not much to put toward our own house."

"It's still three thousand more than we would get if all I did was teach school," said Fred. "There's not even a decent living in that, let alone a home of our own."

"I get scared, Fred," said Barbara, staring out at the rainy night. "When your mother left us that money, she meant it to be security. Is it right to gamble it all on building houses that maybe won't sell? Fred, maybe we'll lose it all."

Fred crossed the unfinished hardwood floor and put his arms

tight about her. "Darling," he said, "you can't be scared. If people get scared, their dreams never come true. And we've done a good job. Best materials, best contractors for the stuff I couldn't do. We didn't skimp on anything. And we've worked hard. Hold on a bit longer. You're the one I count on, you know."

"I know. It's just so frightening to have all you own, Fred, staked on a gamble. I wish we'd sell it quick. The suspense gets me." She cuddled against the soft place low in his neck, and his chin was rough on her forehead. "Fred, I wish this were our home. I've come to love it so."

"We'll have a big house someday. The best I can build. It won't be long, Barbara. Maybe one more house after this will get us enough to start us."

"I hope the people who buy this will love it too. I'd hate to sell it to someone who thought it was just another house."

"All house buyers are stinkers. They'll probably be crabs and complainers and stuck-up and have warts under their eyes. But if they'll just buy it, who cares?"

"I care," said Barbara, running a blistered hand through her short red hair. "I care!"

At three o'clock Sunday, when the sun was bright on the puddles, Mr. Crosby, the real-estate agent, drove down Sweetfern Road and turned into the freshly laid driveway between the concrete blocks and flagstones. In his car, much to his dismay, were not only Cathy and Jim, but baby Deirdre and the two boys, a stuffed elephant, and two space guns. For a month he had driven them to see split levels and old barns, estate cottages, Tudor houses and colonials, ranches with expansion attics. Thirty-three houses he had shown them. Every one had been wrong, even he could see that. Too big, too small, too expensive, taxes too high, no school facilities——

"This, as you can see, is almost completed," said Mr. Crosby. "It has four bedrooms and the usual downstairs. Handsome house."

"How much?" asked Jim, staring at it.

"Two dollars," said one spaceman.

"Sixty-sixty-sixty," said the other.

"Asking thirty-two," said Mr. Crosby.

Cathy looked away from the weather vane and the cupola, down into a puddle.

"But they'll take less," said Mr. Crosby. "Got to. Can't afford to wait out the winter."

"Let's see it," said Jim, his eyes already appraising the double shingles, the steel cellar door, the sturdy shutters, the clean, dignified lines, ferreting out the white stakes that marked the bounds of the property.

The boys stayed outside in the mud. Deirdre toddled over the unfinished floors. Jim and Cathy walked through the house, their faces studiously unenthusiastic. Cathy saw the knotty-pine cabinets, the ceramic-tiled baths, the sliding-door closets, the night light built into the upstairs hall. Jim saw the copper plumbing, the heating system, the insulation in the attic, the pump in the cellar.

Months before, they had concocted a questionnaire of vital information, 36 points they now knew by heart. In flat tones they ran through the list with Mr. Crosby. Taxes? Heating cost? Capacity of fuel tank? Type of septic tank? Capacity of well? Wiring for appliances?

Casually, Mr. Crosby answered. He studied their faces, the settled calm in Cathy's usually mobile eyes, the rigid lines of Jim's chin. Thirty-three houses he had shown them, and never had they looked so disinterested. He had seen yearning on their faces before—for that $40,000 stone ranch, listing ✳2365. And disapproval—for ✳3700 with the jerry-built floors. But never before this mask of nonchalance.

He cleared his throat. "Think I'll drive over and see if I can find Fred Bennett, the builder. He can answer your questions better'n me. You folks stay here. Be right back."

Alone in the bare dining room, with only the hanging light fixture to see them, Cathy and Jim faced each other.

"It's a lovely house."

"Ummm."

"Room enough."

"Well built."

"Land."

"Nice location. School near. Cellar big enough for a play-room someday."

"Guess it's too much. Out of the question."

Jim looked into Cathy's eyes and took her into his arms. "You like it?"

From the corner of his serge lapel, she answered, "Jim, it's so like home should be."

They squatted on the stairs where the balustrade flared outward, and Jim produced his thick black pencil and his black notebook. While he figured and added and balanced and divided, Deirdre toddled happily up and down the bottom step.

"Bet this Bennett guy is a stinker. Builders always are. They don't care about anything in the world but money," said Cathy.

Jim grunted. "We said twenty-five was our limit. But we could go to twenty-six. Not a penny higher."

At five o'clock that Sunday Barbara and Fred Bennett were at one end of the living room, standing near a sawhorse by the porch door. Jim and Cathy were at the other end, by a window, leaning on the sill. Mr. Crosby was in the middle, near the fireplace.

For twelve minutes by Cathy's watch the men had talked about the chance of frost, Sunday traffic on the Merritt Parkway, and the best way to battle hornets. She stole a glance at Barbara Bennett, and blushed when their eyes met. She looked at the baseboard heaters and wondered how long it could take men to start talking business. Deirdre was eating animal crackers. There was no way to heat a bottle here. The boys were in the garage, and she remembered seeing paint there. White paint for the second coat on the doors. It was time they were on the way home. And she could not stand to be in this house any longer, just waiting to know that they could not afford it.

Mutely she appealed to Mr. Crosby.

"Well, now," said Mr. Crosby, rubbing his hands as if a log blazed in the fireplace.

"Well," said Fred Bennett.

"Well," said Jim. "About the house."

Silence.

"How much do you want for it?" asked Jim, with his best courtroom authority.

"I was asking thirty-two," said Fred firmly.

"Now, Fred," said Mr. Crosby.

"We were thinking," Jim said slowly, "of twenty-six. So I guess we'd better forget it." He turned slightly toward Cathy, but he was alert only for Fred's reaction.

"Mr. Crosby said you couldn't go so high. But twenty-six is out." Fred looked at Jim carefully. "I think you really want to buy this house. I want to sell it. But not for twenty-six. Now let's see what we both can do."

The men nodded at each other. This was the way to do it, each thought with relief, no fencing about, all the cards on the table. Mr. Crosby shook his head and pursed his lips. This wasn't the way at all, he wanted to say.

Fred sat down on the sawhorse, and with his chewed green pencil he began to set out the figures he knew so well, carefully, as on a school blackboard.

Barbara bent close to his ear. "Don't you dare give in too far. They've got plenty of money, I bet, no matter what Crosby says." He heard the quiver of fear even in her whisper, and his chin hardened as he leaned over the notebook.

Across the room Jim closed his notebook and rocked on his heels.

"They're out for all they can get," said Cathy in an undertone. Jim tried to see into her eyes, but he could not. A muscle in his cheek twitched.

The sawhorse scraped on the floor. "I could do it for twenty-nine," said Fred, and his voice was a bit cagier than before.

The two women looked at each other across the silence, and the men felt the hostility between them, and their backs stiffened, and the air in the room was stifling. Deirdre squatted by the fireplace, chewing animal crackers at Mr. Crosby's feet. Everyone watched her.

"Twenty-nine," repeated Fred.

Jim cleared his throat. "I might make it twenty-seven five."

"You couldn't buy a house half as good for that price," said Fred. "If you knew anything about houses——"

Jim's eyes narrowed. "Don't tell me about houses. And don't try and tell me what I can pay."

The men glared at each other. Mr. Crosby, who had been counting the stones in the fireplace, flushed at the anger in their voices and stepped forward in conciliation without quite knowing what to say.

In the back of the house the kitchen door opened, and the boys came inside, giggled, and went back out. The door slammed, and the sound echoed through the bare rooms.

Cathy pulled Jim aside, toward the dining room. "Jim, don't fight."

"You're the one who wanted me to be firm."

"Just say no, and we'll get out. Let's go quick, Jim. I don't want to stay here. I—oh, if we can't have it, let's go."

Jim looked at her, and he said, "Cathy," and then he walked back into the center of the living room, away from her, without looking back.

Cathy stood alone by the window, and suddenly her back ached from standing. She wondered wildly what would happen if the baby suddenly decided to be born here, now. She felt a little dizzy, and hungry, and she wanted to laugh.

Then she looked and saw Barbara, also alone, by the porch door, Fred no longer at her side. Barbara's red hair made her face seem pale in the twilight, and tired. The two women's eyes met, and the suspicion between them gave way as they waited to see what their men would do. And they both knew, without being able to say it, that this was a thing for men to do alone, and for women to wait out alone, and they were friends in waiting.

The men were about three feet apart, standing with their weight back on their heels and their hands in their pockets. "If

I take twenty-eight-five, I don't even clear three thousand on the deal," said Fred.

Jim's face was pale, and his eyes were the blue of a winter dawn. "I can make it twenty-eight. But we don't have more than that."

Mr. Crosby stepped forward till he found the exact center floor board of the room. "Well, now," he said, "why don't you folks just split the difference? You each give two fifty and make it twenty-eight thousand two fifty and you got yourselves a deal. Mighty fine deal."

Cathy's knuckles were white.

"Okay by you?" asked Jim.

She looked up, wondering what to answer, but he wasn't asking her. He was asking the man who built this house, the man who sweated over it and shaped it and breathed life into it, the man who loved it as they loved it. It was, thought Cathy wildly, like asking a father for his daughter in marriage.

The man who built it stood and took the measure of the man who wanted to buy it, and a pulse in his cheek was throbbing.

"Okay by me," said Fred Bennett, and his voice was hoarse.

The kitchen door banged open, and the boys brought winter in with them. Their jackets and faces were white with paint, but the cold and the freshness of the outdoor air clung to them and smelled of evening.

"Close the door," said Cathy. "Go back and close the door."

"Yeah. It's your house now," said Jim, "and you've got to learn to close doors. Keep the heat in."

"You gonna buy it, Daddy?"

Jim nodded.

"Oh, boy! Let's go back to our hide-out in the garage." And they ran away, a trail of dried mud behind them.

"Well, I guess it's all settled," said Mr. Crosby. "We'll get all the papers drawn up."

They didn't hear him.

On one side of the room, by the sawhorse, Fred was talking to Barbara. "You wanted someone who loved your house," he said. "And we don't have to wait all winter for our money. We can start on another house soon. We didn't do as well as we hoped, but——"

"But somehow," whispered Barbara, "it'll be all right." She looked at Deirdre, all crumby-gummy with crackers. "I'm glad it's them. I think it was meant to be."

On the other side of the room by the window, Jim and Cathy were whispering too. "Don't ask me how we'll do it," he said. "But we got married on no money. We can buy a house on no money. We can do without any new furniture, can't we?"

Cathy smiled. "We'll do it. And they need the money. I'm glad it's them." She opened her eyes wide and blinked. "We bought a house? What have we done? Jeepers!"

Barbara and Fred heard her and laughed. "And we sold one. Strange feeling, isn't it?"

They left their corners and came together and grinned un-
certainly.

"Well, now," said Mr. Crosby.

Barbara and Fred and Cathy and Jim looked at one another,
and then they all laughed.

"Well, now," said Fred. "Guess we'd better put a 'sold' sign
out front. I can paint one in two minutes, if the boys help me."

By nine that night Cathy and Jim, back again in the city,
had told their mothers the news and were already busy clearing
the coffee table to draw up floor plans and devise a new budget.

By nine fifteen Mrs. Sargent and Mrs. Peabody were on the
phone, drawn together by this new crisis.

"They made up their minds in such a hurry," said Mrs.
Peabody. "I wonder if they did the right thing."

"They spent much more than they planned," said Mrs.
Sargent, as the birds stirred in their cages. "It sounds a bit
strange to me, the way they describe it. All that mud outside——"

"They don't make much sense about it," said Mrs. Peabody.
"They're such kids to be buying a house."

And the mothers riffled through their memories and their
dreams and tried to fit this new idea into place, and they told
themselves to keep hands off their children's lives, and they
worried and grew lonely in the dark.

And that night at eleven the moon shone full on the big
white house behind the stone wall on Sweetfern Road, and

the frost-tongued wind teased the weather vane on top of the cupola on the garage.

The sign outside was white, with big black letters: "SOLD."

But on the house itself there was no visible sign of the hopes and the fears and the loves that had built it and would mold it in the years to come, of the lawns and the swings and the barbecue, the playpens and the dog bones and rosebushes and tomatoes, the treasure hunts and trick-or-treats, the garden parties and the courtings, the daisy dreams and the twilight tears, and the first stars to be wished on.

14. Like an M.C. who has presented his audience with a fine piece of entertainment, I must now come back to wind up the show.

I don't claim that April's is a great story, and for all I know, it isn't Art. It is a good first story, and it sold to one of the world's top magazines, whose editor is famous for his judgment of fiction. To the new writer who wants to sell his first story I would like to point out that it is an expression of the writer's own personality, richness of spirit, and interest in her fellow man. In the very nature of things, these will grow. She'll have more to say and it is plain that she will learn to say it more simply and movingly with experience. Above all, she has used the people and circumstances of her own full, busy young life, so like the lives of many of her readers, for her material. This is, I believe, true of 85 per cent of the great writers. Once more, and again and again and again, I recommend it as a starting point.

O. Henry took a city, where he lived and worked, he took its simplest people, its everyday events, gems of the purest ray serene. I have heard tell that in some quarters these are under an academic eclipse such as Kipling once lived through. I advise you to escape such precious and pretentious affectation and derive all the inspiration you can from seeing what O. Henry accomplished with a little shopgirl who had a picture of Kitchener on her wall; with the guilty party, who sat on the steps of a tenement; with Kid Brady, who wanted to give his girl a fur neckpiece. True, sometimes he's contrived, careless, even a little empty. Even then his sheer gift of telling a story holds you spellbound. At his best he is the perfect storyteller, and above all, he has the priceless gift, the consummation devoutly to be prayed for, striven for, struggled after day and night—he saw, heard, felt stories in everything around him. My son Mac, who is editor of *The Hollywood Reporter*, makes his reporters read O. Henry and try to find as many stories in Hollywood as he did in New York—there ought to be more.

Come down to it, Albert Payson Terhune spoke with dogs, and he didn't do bad telling about *them*.

Sarah Orne Jewett, who wrote the immortal *Country of the Pointed Firs* and so greatly influenced Willa Cather, is often called the best of local-color writers. Which means the same thing as writing about what is around you, making use of the color of your dawns, the girls and boys and old ladies you know, the telephone poles or palm trees or skyscrapers that stretch against your sky.

I don't say that genius can't go away into deep solitude and there alone create great masterpieces. I simply say that it hasn't been done often. Not often enough to be considered as a teachable method of how to write and sell a story. I do say that on the whole, great stories have been produced in the tortured simplicity of hard-working, striving careers by professional storytellers of integrity and humility.

Genius, like everything else, is known by its fruits. Story writing becomes an art, as do all other creative processes, by love, hard work, interest, aspiration, hope, and prayer.

I was talking to Leo McCarey the other day, one of the few people I've ever known about whom I would use that word genius. You probably remember that he directed *Going My Way*, among other Academy Award winners. At the time when a very youthful Leo decided to enter the motion picture art and industry his father, the famed Uncle Tom McCarey who promoted the early championship fights in California, said to him, "Leo, I cannot give you any advice to speak of because I do not know much about the movies. However, I think it might be well to avoid boring people as much as possible."

This re-emphasized what to me is a must.

I have omitted certain writers, certain kinds of writers, because they bore me. Be careful of the "arty" approach to your work. No man can say self-consciously that he is now about to produce Art. He can just give his best, his *all*. Beware of the story called great only, apparently, because nobody can figure out what it's about or supposed to say or where it begins and ends. For secretly you will find that the major sin of this genre of story is that it is as boring as a bunch of artificial orchids or a cold heating pad.

Art grows. It is a living thing. Writing must be a living thing, growing from the heart and soul of the writer. Many will never achieve it. But to produce any honest, real writing is a great career, a fine profession, a service to mankind, and a magnificent life. More vital than any other life I know except that of a truly dedicated minister of God.

Remember, we writers have kept the story of humanity and its struggle toward the light above from generation to generation, century to century. It's a terrific thing to be a writer, a soul-shaking obligation. So good luck and God bless you if you *try*.

And only the Master shall praise us, and only the Master shall
    blame;
And no one shall work for money, and no one shall work for
    fame;
But each for the joy of the working, and each, in his separate star,
Shall draw the Thing as he sees It for the God of Things as
    They Are!

Kipling, the best of them all, knew that.
So must we.
And all these things shall be added unto you.

<u>You can write</u> anywhere <u>or you</u>
<u>can't write. In hotel rooms</u>
<u>with your typewriter on the</u>
<u>washbasin . . . in trains,</u>
<u>planes, press boxes, small,</u>
<u>cold sun porches, kitchens</u>
<u>because that's the only room</u>
<u>you can afford to heat . . .</u>
<u>or the famed attics and</u>
<u>garrets.</u>

HOW TO WRITE
A STORY
AND
SELL IT

by Adela Rogers St. Johns

Here is something altogether
new in "how to write" books
—a down-to-earth, enthusi-
astic discussion with the
outstandingly successful author of more than two hundred
short stories. Adela Rogers
St. Johns, who has been published in every good American
magazine, here draws upon
over forty years of professional experience to deal
with her subject from every
angle—from the problems of
inspiration to the all-impor-
tant process of marketing a
short story.

   Ranging over the whole
field of short-story writing,
Mrs. St. Johns penetrates well
below the surface of the
usual "how to" formula.
Rather than simply presenting
a set of rules to be memo-
rized, she sets off with